WHY POSTERITY MATTERS

For many years the environment has been treated as a free commodity, but it is becoming clear that we cannot continue to exploit it without incurring some cost. Indeed, societies often find that policies which would dramatically improve the welfare of the present population cause severe environmental risks for future generations. This raises moral questions about the relations between people who live in different times, or even different centuries. Avner de-Shalit labels these problems of intergenerational distribution.

Why Posterity Matters argues that our obligations to those who will live after our deaths are a matter of justice and that we must consider them when we make any decisions that will affect their environment. Avner de-Shalit argues that a theory of intergenerational justice is possible and that it can serve as the moral basis for environmental policies.

Utilitarian, contractarian and rights-based theories fail to provide adequate justifications of our obligations to future generations because of their individualistic bases. In *Why Posterity Matters*, a 'communitarian' theory is developed; the concept of a transgenerational community – one which extends into the future – is shown to be morally desirable and justifies a belief in our obligations to future generations.

Avner de-Shalit is a lecturer in environmental ethics and politics at the Hebrew University of Jerusalem. He is the co-editor of a book on communitarianism and individualism and the author of numerous articles on environmental ethics and politics.

ENVIRONMENTAL PHILOSOPHIES
SERIES

Edited by Andrew Brennan

Philosophy, in its broadest sense, is an effort to get clear on the problems which puzzle us. Our responsibility for and attitude to the environment is one such problem which is now the subject of intense debate. Theorists and policy analysts often discuss environmental issues in the context of a more general understanding of what human beings are and how they are related to each other and to the rest of the world. So economists may argue that humans are basically consumers sending signals to each other by means of the market, while deep ecologists maintain that humans and other animals are knots in a larger web of biospheric relations.

This series examines the theories that lie behind different accounts of our environmental problems and their solution. It includes accounts of holism, feminism, green political themes, and the other structures of ideas in terms of which people have tried to make sense of our environmental predicaments. The emphasis is on clarity, combined with a critical approach to the material under study.

Most of the authors are professional philosophers, and each has written a jargon-free, non-technical account of their topic. The books will interest readers from a variety of backgrounds, including philosophers, geographers, policy makers, and all who care for our planet.

Also available in this series

ECOLOGY, POLICY AND POLITICS
John O'Neill

THE SPIRIT OF THE SOIL
Agriculture and environmental ethics
Paul B. Thompson

ECOLOGICAL FEMINISM
Edited by
Karen J. Warren

WHY POSTERITY MATTERS

Environmental policies and future generations

Avner de-Shalit

London and New York

First published 1995
by Routledge
11 New Fetter Lane, London EC4P 4EE

Simultaneously published in the USA and Canada
by Routledge
29 West 35th Street, New York, NY 10001

© 1995 Avner de-Shalit

Typeset in Garamond by
Ponting–Green Publishing Services,
Chesham, Buckinghamshire
Printed and bound in Great Britain by
TJ Press (Padstow) Ltd, Padstow, Cornwall

British Library Cataloguing in Publication Data
A catalogue record for this book is available from
the British Library

Library of Congress Cataloging in Publication Data
A catalogue record for this book has been requested

ISBN 0–415–10018–6 (hbk)
ISBN 0–415–10019–4 (pbk)

*In memory of my father
Amos de-Shalit*

CONTENTS

ACKNOWLEDGEMENTS

I cannot say enough to thank my doctorate supervisor, David Miller, who has been a source of help, criticism and encouragement. I am also indebted to Brian Barry and Michael Freeden for their verbal and written comments. Jerry Cohen, Brian Kney-Paz, Saul Smilansky and Michael Walzer read earlier versions of several chapters and provided fruitful suggestions. My thanks also to Shlomo Avineri and Joseph Raz for intensive discussions of some of my arguments. I also benefited from talks and debates with my colleagues and students. In particular I would like to thank Daniel Attas, Alon Har'el, David Heyd, and my environmental ethics students at the Hebrew University of Jerusalem. I also wish to thank Andrew Brennan for his comments on an earlier draft of this book. Special thanks are due to Gabriel Cohen and Sue Miller for their moral support, and to the owners and workers of Cafe Alexander, Oxford, where many parts of this essay were conceived. Mr. David Maisel helped me editing the manuscript and I thank him for his patience. But most of all, my thanks go to my partner Yifat. Without her support and encouragement this project would never have been finished.

It is a pleasure to acknowledge permission to reprint material from the following sources: 'Environmental policies and justice between generations', *European Journal of Political Research*, 21 (1992); 'Bargaining with the not-yet-born', *International Journal of Moral and Social Studies*, 5 (1990); 'Community and the rights of future generations', *Journal of Applied Philosophy*, 9 (1992). The quotations from Robert Frost are reprinted by the kind permission of Henry Holt and Company, Inc., and Random House UK Ltd.

INTRODUCTION

You, dear future generations, if you are not bigger seekers of justice and peace, if you are not wiser than we are, then go to hell!! Yours, the late Albert Einstein.

Albert Einstein

Development and conservation are equally necessary for our survival and for the discharge of our responsibilities as trustees of natural resources for the generations to come.

The World Conservation Strategy (International Union for the Conservation of Nature and Natural Resources 1980)

Many governments face a new dilemma today. Seeking to improve the welfare of the present population, they find that some of the policies which best do so incur some severe environmental risks for contemporary people, but even more so for posterity. This raises moral questions of relations between generations.[1]

There are two interconnected aspects of relations between generations. One is environmental: we produce pollution and radioactive waste, we destroy rare species of plants, and we deplete non-renewable natural resources. The other is economic: we distribute resources and economic burdens not only among contemporary populations but also between present and future generations. The latter can involve economic actions which at least *prima facie* do not have any environmental aspect. For example, when a government takes a very-long-term loan, its action involves future generations who will have to repay the loan plus interest. But this also applies to economic burdens which are the result of present policies and actions touching on the environment, as when we deplete easily available natural resources leaving future generations with the sole option of utilizing alternative natural resources which are difficult to extract.

1

Now, it is widely acknowledged that we do have certain obligations to future generations: e.g. to consider them when distributing resources, and to refrain from actions such as the unsafe storage of nuclear waste, which could cause them enormous harm. But certain moral issues arise, such as the extent to which we are obliged to consider those living in the future. What, in other words, is the correct principle for evaluating the requirements of both present and future inhabitants of the world? These are questions of distributive justice, but the distribution relates to people who exist in different times, or even different centuries. One can say, therefore, that these are questions of *intergenerational* distributive justice.

In this book it is argued that a comprehensive theory of intergenerational justice is possible and that it can serve as the moral basis for environmental policies. So first let me throw light on the relations between these questions of justice between generations and environmental policies. The two questions that must be tackled are: (a) Why do we need a separate discussion of justice between generations and how does this form of justice differ from justice within a generation? (b) Why shouldn't we be satisfied with the discussion of environmental ethics in terms of the rights or needs of animals, plants, rocks and so forth?

Let me begin by reviewing the issues that such a theory of justice between generations should consider. Generally speaking these issues fall into three categories.

1   The first issue concerns the distribution of access to natural resources in the face of an over-usage of resources. Until recently, this was thought of as an especially urgent issue only in relation to an irreversible depletion of non-renewable resources, such as gas or oil, or the exhaustion of the stock of fossil fuels. Some growth theorists have even rejected the claim that these activities of contemporaries impose heavy burdens on future people, suggesting that future generations could be compensated in terms of knowledge, technology and science. We may deplete oil, they say, but we improve the means of using solar energy. Recently, however, the study of problems of non-renewable resources has been revived and has taken a new direction. It is now acknowledged that the debate should include problems of pollution (which can be seen as an over-usage of clean air, clean water, etc.) and even environmental problems such as the destruction of aesthetically pleasing landscapes.[2]

Thus a theory of justice between generations should consider the following problems: pollution of the soil (disposal of industrial waste and urbanization harm the long-term productive capacity of the soil); contamination of water by chemicals and radioactive materials; endangering certain species of marine life to the point of making them extremely rare in the future; extermination of animal species through the massive use of pesticides; elimination of wild animals in the rain forests; deforestation and the destruction of vegetation; rapid urban development irrespective of a *prima facie* duty to preserve the overall character of ancient cities such as Rome, Athens or Jerusalem; the greenhouse effect caused by an increased carbon dioxide production, the release of methane from rubbish dumps and agricultural and other sources, and the release of nitrous oxide from power stations, car exhausts and agricultural chemicals; air pollution and the phenomenon of 'acid rain'; the use of nuclear energy and problems of radioactive waste; the damage to the ozone layer by our usage of CFCs and carbon dioxide. I shall later elaborate on this last question within the context of intergenerational relations.

2   The second category includes problems arising from budgets with huge deficits or long-term debts and, on the other hand, savings for the sake of future generations. This is not the place to discuss purely economic matters such as a preference for long-term loans over short-term loans with lower interest rates, or the setting aside of large sums of money and their investment in productive enterprises: policies which are very beneficial for the future, but which might contradict the immediate needs of contemporaries. However, this economic aspect of intergenerational relations extends even further, and includes the economic consequences of environmental policies. We are going to leave to future people a world heavily loaded with nuclear weapons and polluted by toxic gases. In order for future generations to eliminate all or any of these, they will have to invest a huge fortune of money and time, which is clearly a potential burden for them.

For many years the environment has been treated by most people as a free commodity. But it is becoming clear (even to politicians) that in the near future we will not be able to use the environment without incurring economic cost. The demand for natural resources, clean air and clean water has been increasing, and will continue to do so. According to a study made by the Hudson Institute, the estimated world energy consumption in 2025 will be 3.4 times greater than it was in the 1980s, and will double itself by 2075 (Kahn 1977). On the other hand, the massive and irresponsible use of natural resources has reduced the amount available for consumption. In the future, people will not literally be charged fees for breathing clean air, but in many places they will 'pay' by breathing polluted air. Some economists argue that in fact the environment should be 'priced' like many other commodities. This, they hope, will help reduce present consumption; but it will not solve the problem completely, because although consumption may decline, depletion will continue, albeit perhaps more gradually. In these circumstances, if the environment is priced, future prices will be high because non-renewable resources become rare, to the degree that they are used. It will thus be fairly expensive to maintain a clean environment in the future. For example, in a report on future environmental needs, S.F. Singer estimated that pollution control costs in the year 2025 would constitute more than 5 per cent of the gross national product of the USA, compared with less than 2 per cent in the early 1970s (Kahn 1977: 149).

3   The third category is population policies. This is an important aspect of intergenerational justice when one considers the ever-growing demands of future generations for energy, food, shelter, clothing, etc. However, I shall not concentrate on this issue here, as it has been widely discussed elsewhere.[3]

Now, one may justifiably ask: is it necessary to have a separate theory of justice between generations? Can we not tackle questions of intergenerational relations with the same principles of justice as we use within one generation? In what way is the issue of justice between generations distinguished from questions of distribution within one generation? I shall not argue that the issue of justice between generations requires a fundamentally novel kind of theory, different from a theory of justice within one generation. However, I claim that this issue raises new problems and difficulties for some theories of justice, difficulties that did not crop up in discussions of justice within one generation. These difficulties derive from some characteristics of intergenerational relations which are absent in the context of justice within one generation. Thus, intergenerational relations differ from relations within one generation in several ways (cf. Narveson 1978).

1 With regard to intergenerational transfers one has to take into account that – assuming there is technological progress – con-

temporary resources are replete with future productive potential. Therefore a transfer of goods from one generation to another generation implies that the latter is likely to receive greater value than the former gives up. For instance, if one generation saves $100 for the sake of another instead of spending it, and if the real growth of productivity is at the rate of 2 per cent per annum, then the other generation will get much more than $100 in terms of real value.

2 Some theories of justice are based on, or refer to, conceptions of needs or preferences. Even theories about welfare rights refer to what people might need. Now, in the intergenerational context, it may be impossible to predict the needs or preferences of future people. And even if those needs or preferences are predictable, it may be over-complicated to compare them with the needs or preferences of contemporaries, which are different and presumably more modest.

3 Our economic transactions with the future are all one-directional. We save for them, we impose economic burdens on them, but they cannot respond, or 'punish' us in economic terms.

4 The size of future populations is unknown. When dealing with the future, we do not know whether we are talking of fourteen or 140, or perhaps 14,000 generations, nor can we predict the average size of a future generation. Moreover, the very existence of future generations depends on our actions today, and theoretically we can decide not to reproduce. On the other hand, in the one-generational context, the size of the population is more or less given, or at least can be estimated. In the intergenerational context there are consequently questions of population which can affect patterns of distribution. Conversely, patterns of distribution affect the size and identities of future populations (Parfit 1984: 361–4).

5 Finally, another characteristic of intergenerational relations is that many actions taken now are irreversible. For instance, if we hunt all African elephants, they will simply disappear. Radioactive waste, once produced, is there and cannot be destroyed. CFCs released into the atmosphere now will damage the ozone layer in thirty to eighty years; once these gases are released there is no way to 'capture' them again, and once the ozone layer is damaged it cannot be reproduced. This feature of irreversibility affects the question of the nature of our obligations to future generations.

All these features will be discussed below. However, one further comment is in order before we go on. Questions of the environment affect contemporaries as well as future generations. Why, then, should we discuss them in terms of obligations to future generations, which are not yet born, rather than to contemporaries? My answer is that we have not considered *all* aspects of environmental policies if we do not address the question of the distribution between generations and our obligations to future generations, in addition to that of distribution among contemporaries. While it is true, for instance, that the destruction of a rare species of animal in the rain forests affects contemporaries (as well as itself, or ecosystems – see below), a consideration of the intergenerational aspects of the case touches other important aspects of the problem. Suppose that you prove to me that although some contemporaries suffer from particular policies with regard to the rain forests, such as deforestation, a greater number of present-day inhabitants of our world benefits from the consequences of these policies. Thus, you may claim, we should allow a limited deforestation. Nevertheless, I reply, your moral duty is to consider how your policies affect the interests, needs, or wishes of future generations. Having done this, actions that appear justifiable in a purely contemporary context appear unjustifiable when future generations are taken into account. Moreover, sometimes the needs or interests of contemporaries come into conflict with those of future generations. It is in such cases that the question of distribution between generations is of crucial importance.

Thus Lawrence Johnson (1991: 149) has recently described the situation in a somewhat oversimplified manner: 'Whatever my attitude toward foreigners, it would be wrong of me to send one a letter-bomb. Would it not also be wrong to send posterity a time bomb?' Actually, relations between generations are more complicated than sending a letter-bomb to a foreigner. In the latter case one has no benefit from sending the letter except, perhaps, for the sadistic pleasure of harming others. But in our context the moral dilemmas derive from the very fact that the harm caused to future persons is the byproduct of a genuine, albeit sometimes mistaken, desire to improve (in terms of a certain ideology) the standard of living of contemporaries.

These features of intergenerational relations already constitute a strong case for constructing a theory of intergenerational justice, which is deserving of a separate discussion. Indeed, it is widely acknowledged that a number of scholars, although aware of the various features of the intergenerational relationship, have failed to adapt their theories of justice in one generation to the new context. I would make an even stronger claim, however: I believe that there is another important reason for advancing a theory of intergenerational justice, which has to do with what is now called 'environmental ethics'. In fact, the most important element in the question of intergenerational justice is the environmental issue,[4] to which almost every aspect of intergenerational relations is related.

Nevertheless, the environmental issue has not always been discussed in terms of distribution between generations. Instead, many have considered the environment in terms of the rights of animals (Goodpaster 1978; Regan 1983), plants (Stone 1972) or monuments, or their welfare (e.g. Singer 1979). The philosophical dilemma arose when people began discussing the moral questions raised by environmental issues. It immediately became clear that the scope of moral and political philosophy not only extended to issues that arise among humans, but also to issues involving humans and animals, humans and natural resources, humans and historical sites or beautiful landscapes, and humans and vegetation. Some scholars have suggested a change in the way philosophers should consider ethics. 'We were following premises of anthropocentric philosophy', they said, 'while we should have followed biocentric premises. Man is not alone at the centre of the universe, but rather man, animals, the vegetation and the environment in general stand there together'. Thus, philosophers have written about animals' rights and the rights of trees; some have even attributed rights to rocks. In general this attitude has been placed under the heading of 'Respect for Nature'.[5]

It is not the purpose of this essay to deny the value of the biocentric outlook and its role as a catalyst in the debate on ecology and morality. On the contrary, the biocentric philosophy is one of the most important 'innovations' of moral and political thought in the last two decades. However, the biocentric approach usually requires us to accept that animals and – according to some scholars – plants have a good of their own, and hence an intrinsic value; or even, it is sometimes argued, moral rights. But it is an empirical fact that many find it difficult to concede that animals, let alone plants, possess moral rights in the same way as humans. The immediate result is that the biocentric philosophers expend a tremendous amount of energy attempting to persuade their audience to accept the biocentric methodology rather than discussing the actual moral obligations of conservation. Thus, those who are sceptical of biocentrism may fail to see the moral grounds for conservation or for 'green' policies, or it may be too late before they realize the validity of the environmentalists' concerns. But these same people may find it easier to see these concerns as representing the moral obligations of contemporaries to future generations, or, in other words, as a matter of just intergenerational distribution. They would then be able to consider the environmental issue within the framework of moral relations among human beings.[6] Thus environmental issues can be discussed as a matter of distribution of access to goods (natural resources, forests, clean air, as well as capital and information) among people of generations which are different and sometimes far apart. Such a theory of justice between generations will have to strike a balance between our obligations to future generations and our obligations to contemporaries, in particular the needy.

Let me say a few more words about the environmental issue as a question of *intergenerational* justice. Access to the enjoyment of the environment – for example, an atmosphere free of CFCs, protected by a reliable ozone layer – is by no means distributed fairly between ourselves and the people of the future. A clean environment, clean water and so forth are only partly renewable, and renewing them will cost future generations a great deal. For instance, the number of reported incidents of water pollution in England and Wales rose from 12,500 in 1980 to 21,095 in 1986–7, and is likely to rise even more with time. If nothing is done now to stop water contamination, future generations will have to allocate huge amounts of money to cleaning water resources. The same applies to global air pollution: if we do not drastically reduce the amount of toxic gases released into the atmosphere, future generations will suffer seriously from birth defects precipitated by foetal absorption of chemicals disrupting the normal development of foetuses. By the same token, at least thirty to fifty years will have to elapse from the time we reduce the amount of acid rain to a reasonable level before lakes and rivers can fully recover from the damage already done. Cleaning the environment, then, is going to be very expensive for future generations – and not only in the financial sense – if the problem is neglected now.

Another option for future generations will be to develop new technologies, such as wind-farms and solar energy, to compensate the depletion of energy resources by previous generations and to avoid further pollution of the environment. But then again, these future generations will have to invest in comprehensive scientific and technological research. One solution commonly proposed nowadays is the recycling of paper, oil products and so on, thereby reducing the depletion of some natural resources and helping to solve problems such as one which a few states in the United States will be facing in the near future, when there will be no room left for dumping rubbish. But in many cases recycling costs more than dumping the rubbish, again raising the question of intergenerational justice: should contemporaries pay more (by subsidizing recycling) for the sake of future people?

A hotly debated form of pollution is that caused by radioactive waste and nuclear accidents. Many experts and governments used to believe that nuclear energy would be cheap for contemporaries and would solve questions of pollution and depletion of resources. This assumption is now challenged. Moreover, according to a recent report by John May (1989) there have been more than fifty nuclear accidents or 'events' in the last forty-five years. Accidents, however, are not the only problem with radioactivity: once nuclear power is produced, so is nuclear waste. Usually the waste is buried, 'wrapped' in three layers – in glass, which is put in stainless steel, which is shielded in bedded salt deposits. For reasons of safety radioactive waste is usually buried in areas which have never suffered earthquakes. But this may still cause a problem for future generations, because our ability to predict earthquakes in places where they have never happened is very poor. Thus, although these areas are not very likely to suffer earthquakes, if one does occur, it will be impossible for future scientists to notify the future local inhabitants in advance and prevent catastrophes. Future people may suffer even if there are no earthquakes, because we have no assurance that the storage of the radioactive waste will indefinitely prevent leaking.

The problem of damage to the ozone layer is another illustration of the fact that environmental issues are a matter of relations between generations. The gases known as CFCs are cheap and widely employed in aerosol spray cans and refrigerators, to mention but two uses. But since 1974 scientists have been concerned that the continued release of these gases will lead to damage to the ozone layer, which is vital to maintain life on earth because it serves to filter out dangerous solar radiation. It takes a very long time – about thirty years – for CFCs released on the earth's surface to rise up through the atmosphere to the ozone layer. Once there, they will be active for several decades. This suggests that the people most likely to suffer from the chemical effects of our use of CFCs are those who will be living in sixty to eighty years from now.

Should we then immediately stop using CFCs? What about people who live now and benefit from them? After all, these gases are very cheap and safe for contemporary people. Those nations that are only now introducing refrigerators (China for example) argue that they must supply the already existing stock of refrigerators with CFCs because they have no alternative means for supplying refrigerators. Here again, obligations to future generations seem to conflict with the interests of (some) contemporaries.

The list of such examples is almost inexhaustible. We could go on to discuss the greenhouse effect, the rise of the sea level, the destruction of beautiful landscapes and historical sites (Clark 1986; de-Shalit 1994), all of which will occur and affect future generations unless we in the present day rein in our consumption. Indeed, the examples I have discussed here have all been situated in the context of relations between human beings, as matters of distribution between different generations, because environmental issues are essentially concerned with intergenerational distribution of access to resources. If resources are defined broadly, so as to include even landscapes, then environmental policies need not be couched in terms of the rights of rocks or monuments, but rather in more traditional terms of distributive justice. Governments, political theorists and the public-at-large should therefore realize that any conception of distributive justice cannot neglect the effects of the present distribution of resources on the distribution in the future, or on the distribution of resources between the present and future generations. In the final analysis, environmental problems are social and political and can be solved politically, with the help of political theory. This book, then, is an attempt to find the philosophical justification of environmental, or 'green' policies.

However, when we talk of intergenerational justice and obligations to future generations, it is not quite clear what we mean by these obligations. Do we suggest saving money, or perhaps investing now for the sake of the yet unborn? Do our obligations to future generations require the conservation of all species? Are contemporaries morally obliged never to destroy any beautiful building because of duties to posterity? Or can we occasionally develop some areas even at the risk of damaging historical monuments? Do our obligations to posterity extend to all future generations or do they 'fade away' in the remote future? Let me say, then, a few words about obligations to future generations.

There are those who believe that the aim of philosophy is to bring light to those who remain in the cave-like darkness. My aim in this book, however, is more modest: to justify or to discover the moral grounds for an intuition most of us share about our obligations to future generations and about intergenerational justice. This intuition is common to many people, although not to everyone. In the last five years I have discussed the issue with many friends and colleagues. Most of them have agreed with me about our obligations to future generations. Indeed, many environmentalists, Greens, socialists, many liberals – perhaps even some conservatives – concur with me in these beliefs. However, before I describe these obligations, I should point out that some people deny that we have any obligations to future generations, while others think our obligations to future generations are much more far-reaching than those I have in mind. The latter group includes some 'deep' Greens, who believe that only by giving absolute priority to conserving the environment over, say, industrialization can our obligations to future generations be fulfilled.

This book puts forward the view that, although future generations are by definition people who will live after our deaths, our obligations to them are a matter of *justice*, rather than of charity or supererogation. It is therefore our duty to consider them when we distribute access to resources and when we plan our financial policies and budgets. Our obligations, however, are not infinite or boundless. When obligations to future people conflict with a genuine need to improve the welfare of contemporaries, a middle way has to be found. In general, we have very well-founded and definite obligations to immediate future generations, e.g. those up to eight or ten generations from now. Such obligations imply conservation policies. In contrast, our obligations to remote future generations – for instance, thirty generations from now – are less definite and well-defined. When these obligations to very remote future generations do not contradict obligations to contemporaries, we have no excuse not to fulfil them. But if these obligations to very remote future generations clash with certain obligations to contemporaries, and especially to the worst off among our contemporaries, it is reasonable to argue that in some cases our obligations to contemporaries have some priority (although this difference by no means cancels out our obligations to very remote future generations).

My contention is that the utilitarian, contractarian, and rights-based theories fail to provide justifications for our obligations to future generations. But, at the same time, there is no need to jump to hasty conclusions, such as Derr's (1981), that only a religious perspective can provide a morality relevant to intergenerational justice. Hence, I shall begin by putting forward a 'communitarian' theory of intergenerational justice, which is based on a conception of human beings seeking a moral environment transcending self-interest. Analysing the concept of a *transgenerational* community' – one that extends *into the future* – I argue that it reflects this conception of the person, that it is morally desirable, and that it justifies a belief in obligations to future generations. I also analyse the limitations on the transgenerational community and their implications for our theory. I shall then go on to explain why the above theories fail to do the job.

In the final chapter I shall discuss the implications of our obligations to future generations, although only briefly, because my main aim in this book is to establish the moral grounds for these obligations rather than to determine their precise content. The essay concludes with a short review of the questions that remain to be answered. I do not claim to have resolved all questions of intergenerational justice. However, many scholars have expressed puzzlement after discussing the moral grounds for our obligations to future generations. If my essay can shed some light on the matter and help to trace a path to be followed, I shall be satisfied.

1

THE TRANSGENERATIONAL COMMUNITY

Some say the world will end in fire. Some say in ice.
                                    Robert Frost, *Fire and Ice*

INTRODUCTION

Although I call the theory which I shall put forward a communitarian theory, I shall permit myself not to review communitarianism here.[1] But before we begin, let me again express my intuition about the obligations to which I shall be referring. We have, I believe, positive and negative obligations to close and immediate future generations. That is, we should consider them when deciding on environmental policies; we should not overburden them; furthermore, we should supply them with goods, especially those goods that we believe are and will be necessary to cope with the challenges of life, as well as other, more non-essential goods.

The case is different with the very remote future generations: there, our 'positive' obligations (those beyond merely preventing damage, e.g. providing resources) 'fade away', so to speak. To people of the very remote future we have a strong 'negative' obligation – namely, to avoid causing them enormous harm or bringing them death, and to try and relieve any potential and foreseeable distress. Thus we should stop producing nuclear energy, because future generations are likely to suffer because of potential leakages or because of the unsafe storage, we should refrain from depleting natural resources and demolishing aesthetic monuments and spoiling beautiful landscapes, we should stop deforestation, reduce the amount of toxic waste to a minimum, and so on and so forth. This, of course, is something that we owe to every future generation, be it immediate or remote. But the idea of a duty to provide the very remote future generations with many of the goods that we distribute to people of closer future generations is dubious. Of course, this in no way undermines the importance of our 'negative' obligations to remote future generations, which in turn imply some 'positive' policies requiring certain actions.

Now, some may think that there should be no time-limit to our obligations to future generations, arguing that any other notion of intergenerational justice discriminates against very remote future generations.[2] Before considering this question in greater depth (see p. 51), I will point out that a theory of morality, or of applied philosophy (as environmental philosophy is), should not demand what is absolutely impossible. If people are told that they should share natural resources, e.g. coal, with people who will be alive six or twelve generations from now, they will at least listen and may even tend to agree. But if they are told that they should share access to coal with someone living in the year 2993 or 3993, the response will probably be, 'To hell with morality and intergenerational justice! This is ridiculous; such policies do not make any sense because they are inconceivable!' I am not claiming that what people think is always right or moral, but rather that our principles of intergenerational justice should not go beyond what is reasonably intelligible and imaginable. This is important to bear in mind because we are discussing relations with the remote future, which in itself is difficult to conceive.

This raises many questions, among them just what can reasonably be envisaged, so in Chapter 6 I study the implications of the theory that I advance in environmental policies. However, my intuitions, I strongly believe, are common to many people – philosophers, politicians, governmental bodies and 'ordinary' people alike. Indeed, human behaviour indicates that these are the lines along which we believe we should construct a theory of obligations to future generations, and several empirical studies and polls support this claim (O'riordan 1991; Renner 1991).[3]

THE ARGUMENT: OBLIGATIONS AND THE TRANSGENERATIONAL COMMUNITY

Our obligations to future generations derive from a sense of a community that stretches and extends over generations and into the future. Part of what the transgenerational community stands for is the idea of obligations between generations. However, contrary to the conservative concept of community, which looks backwards and sees an obligation to continue the heritage of previous generations, I advance a concept of the transgenerational community that extends into the future and so may appeal to Social Democrats, Greens, Socialists and 'progressivists' in general.[4] My argument may not appeal to those denying any sense of community; those who claim that all moral principles should be based on and derived from universally grounded principles will probably not agree with me. But I find it difficult, if not fruitless, to enter into a debate here.

So I shall accept Aristotle's teaching that he who lives outside the community is 'either too bad or too good, either subhuman or superhuman',[5] or, in other words, non-human. Thus a person is conceived as bound by social connections and relationships, and, among other things, her personality is actually defined by the obligations she has, so that 'to divest oneself of such commitments would be, in one important sense, to change one's identity' (Miller 1988: 650).

I assume, then, that if and when one admits the existence of a community, and if one acknowledges that the community constitutes one's identity, then it is absurd at the same time to deny any obligation to the community and its members. If one acknowledges the importance of the community, then one wishes the community to be sustained, and even to flourish.

> Relations with others are not purely external to the self. My commitment to my friends or my children, to a person whom I love or a social movement in which I believe, may be a part of my own deepest being, so that when I devote myself to them, my overriding experience is not of sacrificing myself but of *fulfilling myself*.
>
> (Norman 1983: 249, emphasis added)

I shall therefore refrain here from attempting a metaphysical justification of the community, or from an exhaustive discussion of the question of why one has obligations if one belongs to a community, and I shall not attempt to prove that obligations derive from membership.[6] Instead I argue that if one accepts the idea of a community in one generation, including the principle that this entails certain obligations to other members, then one should accept the idea of a transgenerational community extending into the future, hence recognizing obligations to future generations. I am claiming here that the constitutive community extends over several generations and into the future, and that just as many people think of the past as part of what constitutes their 'selves', they do and should regard the *future* as part of their 'selves'. These are the relations that form the transgenerational community, which is the source of our obligations to future generations.

For those who tend to take the idea of a community for granted, a transgenerational community should not be such a strange concept. It is, perhaps, an extension of the concept of the community, as applied to one's contemporaries, to a sphere – that of time – which lies beyond one's immediate environment. People who associate radical individualism with some sort of alienation, and who tend to regard the group to which they belong as part of their self-identity and self-understanding, should accept that this group does not necessarily have to be in their 'immediate environment'. For instance, in his criticism of anarchism, David Miller refers to national identity and writes: 'People clearly feel a need to locate themselves in relation to something beyond their own immediate environment' (Miller 1984: 179). But if we interpret 'immediate' not as a geographical description but rather as a temporal one, then the transgenerational community may be regarded as one of these objects that lie beyond one's immediate environment.

However, several interpretations exist of the concept of a community (Plant 1978). And as if this were not enough, I extend the concept to include people who are not yet born. Let me then draw attention to one point which will reduce the number of relevant interpretations of a community: among all the conceptions of a community, those that are acceptable must be compatible with the notion of *free* and *rational* agency.[7] Although sentiments and emotional ties are important elements of a community and should be treated as such, I consider the members of a community to be rational; i.e. they subject their membership in the community to a critical examination. This is a normative requirement rather than an empirical description of a community and, as such, it is perhaps at variance with the more 'historical' (sometimes called 'Aristotelian') approach to membership of a community. 'Historical' communitarians would argue that, in their opinion, I might not be able to reflect upon and change my membership of a community. Thus, their concept of a community is historical: if one was born into a community, one would probably remain in it. In the final analysis, they would say, what binds me to the community is something I 'feel' and acknowledge regardless of rational consideration. However, I shall later be analysing other aspects of membership, no less important, which are subject to criticism and reflection.

We cannot accept a concept of a completely deterministic community – one to which we are born without any possibility of change afterwards – because it could not be compatible with the idea that the community constitutes the self and with the notion of a rational person. Thus the concept of community that I shall use here may rightly be seen as less deterministic than the one used by some scholars, in the sense that I insist on the opportunity, given to every member at any time, to reflect on the community's values, and to try either to alter them or to leave the community and join another if not satisfied. This, as I show below, is a condition essential to the success of a transgenerational community.

Lastly, I refer to obligations to very remote future generations, arguing that these do not derive from communitarian relationships. They are comparable to the feelings of many Westerners that they should try in some way to help the starving people in Somalia, although they do not share any communal relationships with them. (I explore the grounds for these obligations in the section on 'Obligations to remote future generations' in Chapter 2)

LACK OF INTERACTION BETWEEN GENERATIONS

Suppose now that we accept the concept of a community and acknowledge its importance. Nevertheless, we say, what is a transgenerational community? What is the meaning of this concept?

Some may object to the concept because it is indeed not immediately clear that a community extends over generations and into the future. Usually a community is associated with the interaction between the members of that community: they live together, have commercial relationships, and experience the same wars, natural disasters, and so on. If we think of a small community – say, a village – we can imagine the members of this community going swimming together, working together, meeting at the local pub, complaining about the weather, and so forth.

A community, it could be said, is thus a tangible concept only with regard to people who more or less know each other, or who at least could theoretically do so, and the idea is therefore clearly intelligible only when applied to one generation, or perhaps two. But what kind of relationships does one have with someone who will live six generations from now? Can such future people be said to have any interaction with us? How can we speak of a transgenerational community when there does not seem to be any 'real', face-to-face conversation or interaction between the generations?

This argument can be traced in the literature relating to inter-generational justice. Norman Care, for instance, acknowledges the actuality and importance of the idea of the community and does not oppose it. Yet he nevertheless writes:

> If we ask at this point whether motivation in the form of community bonding is available and reliable to support pol-icies designed to implement what morality requires of us on behalf of the world of the future, I think the answer must be no. We (current people) and they (future people) are not positioned in such a way as to be able to reciprocate with each other concerning the constituent ideas and controlling aims of any associations or enterprises which we jointly participate in or endure.
>
> (Care 1982: 208–9)

Thus, Care argues that communitarian relations with future genera-tions are not possible because current people and future people 'are not positioned in such a way as to be able to reciprocate with each other'. In the absence of such an interaction, Care does not see how any feeling of loyalty or sense of being on the same side, all of which are necessary to community bonding, can develop. Furthermore, he says, in our relation to the people of the future we lack any sense of guilt, which usually arises when one fails to follow the prescribed dictates of the communal relationships.

But there is evidence that one is mistaken in denying that such feelings exist. Most writers on the environment, at any rate, refer with deep regret and remorse to the environmental harm we have been causing to future generations, and the consequent burden that we have been placing on their shoulders. How can Care acknowledge certain obligations to future people while denying feelings of guilt when these are not fulfilled? It is also mistaken to claim that relations between the people of the future and ourselves lack the detailed knowledge that at least makes people interesting to one another. There is no lack of science-fictional literature, drama and films that show just how interesting the future and the future inhabitants of the earth are to us. Indeed, one can make the general observation that people are interesting to each other even when they do not interact, and perhaps especially when they do not – witness, for example, the West's fascination with the Tibetans, their religion and their way of life.

Another philosopher who recognizes the concept of a community yet is somewhat sceptical about relations with future generations is M.P. Golding – perhaps the first scholar to write of a community in the context of intergenerational justice, and, indeed, one of the first to deal with the issue as a whole (Golding 1972). And yet, it is not quite clear whether or not Golding genuinely agrees that we are part of the community of future generations, for he writes:

> There is something which is due to *the community of the future* from *us*. ... They [future generations] comprise the community of the future, a community with which we cannot expect to share a common life.

and

> They [the obligations] are owed to an unspecified, and perhaps unspecifiable, community of the future.
> (Golding 1972: 64, 69, 63, emphasis added)

Indeed Golding sees a difficulty here: we do not share a common life with future generations. He also adds a new dimension to the debate: we lack *moral* interaction. The problem is that he is referring to observable interaction, and he is therefore not certain about obligations to future people, who will live after our death.

Now, is Golding right? It is often claimed that the distribution or redistribution of goods within a community is based on the acquiescence of its members, derived from their awareness that together they constitute the community and that the good of the community is also their own good. But this also implies that these people are primarily concerned with the members of that particular community, and seek to distribute the goods – sometimes exclusively – among its members (Walzer 1985: 31). We must therefore ask who the members of our community are. Is our neighbour a member? Are all the citizens of our country members of our community, or perhaps only those whom we like? Or would all the people in the world be members? Were our grandparents members? Suppose you are a member of my community, will your great-grandchildren also be?

The latter question is perhaps the most interesting to emerge from our present discussion, as it raises the problem of whether people from different generations, far apart, can be part of a single community. We have already seen that the sceptics deny any possibility of a transgenerational community because there is no interaction with people who are not yet born. But my argument about the existence of such a community is supported by behavioural indications that we have membership of an association that stretches beyond the present generation, i.e. that we are members of a transgenerational community.

Such behavioural indications abound: we maintain customs practised by previous generations such as religious rites and ceremonies, e.g. baptism in Christianity or circumcision in Islam and Judaism; we marry in approximately the same manner as our ancestors did; in many universities, students attend a matriculation ceremony just as their counterparts did years ago; new parliamentary assemblies are opened in the same way as they have been opened for decades; every year, we hold memorial ceremonies for the soldiers who died in battle and we assert that their deaths served to defend us, although some (or most) of us were not yet alive when they fought and died.

All these customs are part of how we see ourselves and what we see ourselves to be. Baptism is part of being a Christian, i.e. belonging to a certain community; the opening of parliamentary assemblies with a traditional ceremony demonstrates the fact that we belong to the democratic tradition or political current; paying tribute to fallen soldiers who defended us by their death affirms our membership of the same national community. People obviously conceive of the democratic tradition, Christianity, their nation and so on as extending over many generations, and so people do in fact identify themselves with transgenerational communities of values, norms, and ideas. These indications exist in many varied spheres of life: they can be found, for instance, in public and private, religious and secular ceremonies and in traditional political practices. When people behave in a way that indicates more than simple respect to past generations, it seems that their attitude to the past is not only a response to the assumed will of past generations that future people should respect them and their achievements, but also an acknowledgement that the remote past is in a sense an integral part of their identities.

But these indications are not enough, because it might be argued that they are based on subjective feelings. Indeed, the transgenerational community can be viewed from two perspectives: that of the subjective member (the insider) and that of the 'neutral', objective observer (the outsider). The insider asks, 'Do I regard myself as a part of a transgenerational community?' The outsider asks, 'Does a transgenerational community exist?' The two answers are not necessarily congruent, for the insider may have a false consciousness. She imagines a transgenerational community to exist, when the outsider may argue that several conditions are absent. Actually, when they relate to a community, 'outsiders' often have in mind a transgenerational community (e.g. when historians write about the history of the Indians, or about class struggle in England). From the perspective of the outsider, the community remains constant over generations although its members change; people die and others are born, but we continue to speak of the same community: the British Labour party, the Tibetan Buddhists, etc.

Indeed, it may be claimed that this is not a conclusion, but rather a part of the very definition of what a community is: it is more than simply an incidental, random aggregation of members, or a passing episode, or a functional gathering for one purpose. It is therefore quite obvious that, although some people die and others are born, the same community remains, and the essence of that community is continuity and succession. But what about the perspective of the member, the 'insider'? One may well continue to ask, 'Why do I and why should I behave as part of a transgenerational community? Moreover, how is such a membership expressed? If there is no everyday interaction, how is a transgenerational community possible?'

THE TRANSGENERATIONAL COMMUNITY: CULTURAL INTERACTION, MORAL SIMILARITY, AND THE ROLE OF REFLECTION

To answer these questions, we must first look at some characteristics of a community, analyse them, and see what form they take in the multigenerational context. I am interested here in exploring and understanding the elements that transform a group of people into what we call, and they would feel to be, a community, and in particular a transgenerational community.

One way to accomplish this task is by asking ourselves whether the transgenerational community would continue or cease to exist if and when each of its characteristics were removed. If, for instance, we discover that the absence of cultural interaction causes the transgenerational community to degenerate into no more than a fortuitous and insignificant collection of people, then we can assume that cultural interaction is necessary for the existence of a trans-generational community. Moreover, as I hope to show in the next section, the degree to which cultural interaction (as in the above example) extends over generations will also determine the weight we must give to future people when considering their needs or rights in relation to the needs or rights of contemporary people.

One of three main conditions has to be met in order for a group of people to count as a community. These conditions are interaction between people in daily life, cultural interaction, and moral similarity. But we have already seen that the first – interaction in daily life – does not exist in the transgenerational context. Indeed, the argument against the concept of a transgenerational community, which I have described and challenged above, is based on the absence of interaction. This cannot be denied, but on the other hand it must be pointed out, that on the everyday level, interaction is confined to a somewhat limited sphere: it relates to commercial and economic life, to commonplace activities – working, shopping, renting flats, and so forth. These aspects of life can be more adequately described in *non*-communitarian terms even in the context of relations within a single generation. The concept of a community is not a total one in the sense that it leaves room to humans to relate to each other in several ways, some of which are instrumental and non-communitarian (Miller 1989; de-Shalit 1992a). If this is true for relations within one generation, it is certainly so in the context of many generations. However, there is also another very important form of interaction, namely, cultural interaction. So let us now proceed to analyse this concept.

The community and cultural interaction

Let us look, for example, at a citizen of a certain country, say England. As a member of the English nation (let us accept for the moment that a nation is a community) she has been raised on English literature, poetry, theatre, music, drama, and so forth. There are special codes – symbols, types of humour, atmosphere, forms of trauma – that she is familiar with, codes which strangers may find difficult to understand or follow. Moreover, this person has been involved in cultural, social, and political activities and debates through discussions, arguments, participating in elections and demonstrations, signing petitions, and so forth.

Let me elaborate on the argument that a person is raised on his or her community's cultural environment. The cultural environment refers *inter alia* to language in its broad sense, i.e. as including codes and symbols that enrich and vary communication. As Allan Gibbard notes, 'We think as individuals, but, partly too, we think in groups' (Gibbard 1989: 187).[8] A well-known folk-tale demonstrates my point. A man comes to a town he has never before visited. He wanders here and there, until he reaches a place where many people are gathered together. To his surprise, he sees that the crowd listens to one person at a time and then bursts into laughter. As he comes closer he hears one person call 'number 26', and the others respond by laughing. Another person says 'number 45', and the crowd shakes with laughter. Someone else shouts '14' and they all roll on the floor. The stranger decides to try his luck and shouts out 'number 11'. He is greeted with silence. He tries again: '76!', but doesn't even raise a smile. He then calls out '56' but gets no response. He turns to one of the locals and asks, 'Why don't you laugh?' The man looks at him coldly and replies, 'Oh, you don't know how to tell jokes.'

Words, phrases, pauses, stresses – all these are heavy with connotations or associations whose meaning to 'natives', to those familiar with them, is deeper than to outsiders who have never been attuned to them. This is because every community has its own history of cultural interaction. People in a community undergo the same political, social, and cultural experiences; they reflect on and interpret the significance of these events through discussion, literature, the mass media, academic research, and so on. Thus the 'local' literature, poetry, painting and performing arts – theatre, films, television productions – become common property, in the sense that all members of the society are engaged in them in one way or another, either actively participating, or watching, reading, or criticizing.

This does not apply only to nations. Most Marxists, for example, would understand why the hyphen in the term Marxism-Leninism was important, because they are familiar with the concept, the debate about the concept that took place until the 1950s; they know its history, its emotional associations, the arguments connected with it, and so on. 'Outsiders' (non-Marxists) will find it difficult to understand why the hyphen was so crucial. Or when environmentalists hear the concept of Gaia, they not only know that it refers to the planet as a living entity, but they also know that it offers a holistic view of the planet, and that it is connected with the view of earth from space; they associate the concept with Lovelock's book and with the ancient idea of Mother Earth as the nurturing source of life, and they are familiar with the debate on the concept, and perhaps even with Porritt's endorsement of the hypothesis (1984: 207) and with Dobson's critique of it (1990: 42–5). But 'outsiders' will have to ask not only about the concept, but about all these connotations as well.

All this interpretation of local events, this interaction, this 'give and take' between creators and audience and of each party among themselves has an enormous impact on the members of a community. It shapes the way they think, it determines what they think about, and it gives rise to a special language with specific social and historical connotations, which become part of the community and its life. Add to this meaningful ceremonies (such as national memorial days, or academic conferences and the unwritten rules according to which they are conducted) or symbols and symbolic customs (e.g. the Jewish custom of eating unleavened bread at Passover) – add all these and you have a complex cultural interaction between the members of a community.

Moral and political debate is a further element in cultural interaction. A genuine community, as opposed to other social groupings, is one in which the members regard the ideas of the community as constitutive of their identities. Thus, the communitarian vision of politics welcomes members actively involved and engaged in political debate. It is only natural for the communitarian to praise political debate, especially when it is about the idea of the good, about norms and values. If the ideas of the community constitute the identities of its members, then the members ought necessarily to express what they think and feel about these ideas. Hence they are all expected to contribute in one way or another to the public debate.[9]

Those active in such a debate regard the goal of politics as the transformation of an order of preferences through rational discussion, rather than an enumeration of certain preferences, resulting in a compromise.[10] They wish to convince their fellows through a process of open debate of the values, norms, and ideas that should constitute their common public life. They believe that one brings to this debate not interests – at least not only interests – but the very concepts and values which constitute one's 'self'. Moreover, they assume that each participant is capable of being convinced if and when she realizes that the other's argument is cogent. Hence they reject a view of the political debate as one in which each participant has a certain fixed opinion (derived from interests) which she is unwilling to forgo once persuaded she is wrong. Genuine debate comes about when (a) there is a free, active, and substantial exchange of opinion on the idea of the good; (b) there is some broad area of common agreement as a background (mainly on account of a common moral tradition); and (c) there is a desire to reach agreements, not in the sense of a pragmatic compromise but as a result of persuasion. Only then will the ideas of the community be regarded as constitutive of the members' notions of their 'selves'. Now this definition of cultural debate in a transgenerational community may appear too broad, including as it seems every group of people who have an argument. (Palestinians and Israelis, for example, have a history of arguing but obviously do not form a community.) Let me therefore suggest that cultural interaction exists when most, if not all, the members of a community aim at reaching a common set of ideas which determine a common good. (Unfortunately, Palestinians and Israelis fail to meet this condition.) They also relate to this set of ideas as an important element in their personal identities.

Cultural interaction, then, exists when, in addition to the common language, codes, and tradition of symbols, there is a cultural, moral, and political debate. That is when people accept that they are governed by common values and principles, not just by arrangements of political compromise; when moral issues are not excluded from the public discourse because the latter is regarded as more than merely pragmatic reasoning (Benhabib 1989); when politics are seen as a theatre of debate in which the community should decide upon its view of justice, and when people enter the debate not in order to gain power over their fellows, but in order to persuade through instruction and with an openness and readiness to be persuaded.

Moral similarity and reflection

Contrary to the common idea of communitarianism as being too authoritative, lacking in tolerance and so forth, cultural interaction and any genuine public debate must be related to pluralism in society because, without a variety of ideas, no fruitful debate can occur. Nevertheless, cultural interaction is sometimes directed towards the aim of attaining a moral similarity.

As noted above, we usually think of a community as a group of people who see each other often, who have commercial relations, who occupy a common territory – in short, people who experience all kinds of direct interaction. In this 'face-to-face' type of community, it may be argued, it may be this very communication and interaction which holds the community together. But it is possible to imagine a community which lacks this 'face-to-face' characteristic: for instance, Americans regard those who have emigrated from America to other countries for various reasons to be Americans in every sense (with the exception of those who have left because of a rejection of the fundamental principles of the American Constitution). The Democratic Party allocates a few seats in its conventions to Americans who live in foreign countries thousands of miles away, and there are branches of the Democratic Party outside the United States with active members who regard themselves as fully-fledged Americans. Similarly, many Jews in Israel refer to the Jews in the United States, Russia, Ethiopia, and elsewhere as their 'community'. So strong is this belief that the Israeli Government has declared its readiness to spend tens of thousands of pounds on any Jew who decides or obtains permission to emigrate to Israel. The transgenerational community is similarly a community that lacks these 'face-to-face' relations. But what is the feature that makes these groups of people – the American Democratic Party, the Jews or the transgenerational community – into 'communities'? It is, I suggest, the search for moral similarity.

Before proceeding any further, let me say that by analysing the moral similarity of a community I neither intend nor wish to reduce the concept of a community to a package of beliefs and ideas. I must therefore make it clear that moral similarity is one aspect of a community and should not be seen as independent from other aspects. In addition, moral similarity should be distinguished from the idea of unanimous agreement on moral and political questions. Unanimity is very unlikely to be achieved because of different interests and different interpretations of the common good. One can say, then that moral similarity coexists happily with pluralism, and the community must be careful not to fall into the trap of searching for a unanimous agreement, which might lead very quickly to a coercive unity.

Indeed, some people have criticized communitarianism, asking what communitarians would do in the face of unresolved moral conflicts, i.e. cases in which the justifications of both sides are 'internal all the way down' (cf. Lukes 1989: 141). The communitarian answer is that, although some conflicts are of this sort, they should never be resolved by enforcing the morality of one side. But, at the same time, repressing these conflicts by choosing a procedure rather than a debate is not the right solution either. It may serve as a temporary, tactical measure to ensure a continuity of order, but the problem is the moral dilemma itself rather than the fact that we cannot agree upon a solution. Let us take as an example the debate between conservationists and developers. The two sides put forward two conceptions of the good life, and, according to the environmentalists at least, the problem is not that there are certain people (the developers) who have a different view of the good; the trouble is the pollution the developers are creating and the irreversible damage that they are causing to ecosystems, which is not only unwise but also immoral. Here, a unanimous agreement is unlikely and a coercive unity is just as immoral.

On the other hand, moral similarity should be distinguished from what is sometimes called 'cultural homogeneity' when the latter refers to ethnic groups, not necessarily with any moral or political aspirations, and to folklore rather than to moral and political values. There can be several ethnic groups in one nation; they may have several folkloric traditions, e.g. they dance different kinds of dances. What makes them a nation, although there is no cultural homogeneity, is that they all have some norms and values in common – i.e. a moral similarity, which forms them into one entity. (This, of course, is not a definition of a nation, but rather a description of the place of moral similarity within the model of a community.) Now, one should be very careful when discussing cultural homogeneity in this context, because moral similarity can include some cultural aspects. For example, one could describe some English manners (which are, no doubt, part of English culture) as values, and hence as part of the English moral similarity. For instance, people in England tend to finish statements with a question, e.g. 'This is a splendid book, isn't it?' This habit is so rooted in the mode of conversation that it has become part of the way people talk in England, and thus a part of cultural homogeneity. At the same time, it expresses the value of searching for a consensus which has characterized public life in that country for decades. Thus, the habit of ending statements with a question constitutes an aspect of the moral similarity in England. I therefore maintain that we should distinguish between moral similarity and cultural homogeneity when the latter refers to ethnicity and folklore.

We have now seen what moral similarity is not. It is not cultural homogeneity, nor unanimous agreement, nor does it necessarily require face-to-face relationships. What is it, then? In every genuine community some values and some attitudes towards moral and political questions are common to most people and serve as a background or as a framework when the members engage in discourse on their political and social life. These values and attitudes are, in fact, spectacles through which a member looks at the world around her. Each member of the community shares these values, ideas, and norms with the other members. She regards the values as constitutive of her personal identity, and considers them as her own goals and aims as well as those of her community.

When these attitudes, values, and norms are common and more or less accepted, we can talk of moral similarity. In an ideal community, a community that achieves moral similarity, one regards both what one receives from the community and what one has to offer as expressing one's true nature and as integral to one's concept of the self. As Charles Taylor writes:

> The community is not simply an aggregation of individuals; nor is there simply a casual interaction between the two. The community is also constitutive of the individual, in the sense that the self-interpretations which define him are drawn from the interchange which the community carries on.
>
> (Taylor 1985a: 8)

Indeed Taylor thinks that the members of a society are capable of practising certain virtues (e.g. 'autonomy') only in a given community that offers what I call a moral similarity which embraces these virtues. For the practice of autonomy, for example, members need a community that appreciates it, together with an open public debate about moral principles such as autonomy. Hence Taylor adds, 'What we are as human beings, we are only in a cultural community' (1985a: 206–7; 1975: 380).

Moral similarity, then, serves as the background for political debate. However, in the intergenerational context we see that in order to reach moral similarity there has to be some sort of cultural interaction, which may sometimes derive from feelings of 'historical' community. Very rarely do we see a community that is formed as a result of someone saying, 'Friends, we think the same about many issues. Let us form a community!' (The Israeli Kibbutz is a rare example of such a community.)

How, then, do people who are in a state of cultural interaction achieve moral similarity? The process involves questioning and criticism, and thus represents a step forward from the first stage of community – the 'historical' one, in which members regard the community as constitutive of their selves in the sense that they were 'brought up' by the community – to the second stage. This is a more evolved stage in which the sense of belonging is more developed, because people have questioned the necessity for membership and have decided, as a result, that they would like to stay in this particular community, or else have chosen to belong to it – a difficult and irksome choice, but not impossible to arrive at. Thus the process becomes a *rational* one.

The rational process begins when people ask themselves whether the ideas they have been sharing are good ones, whether they tie in with their moral intuitions. Thus, these people become engaged in a debate on ideas – the political debate mentioned earlier. In the course of the debate some new ideas are examined, and others are found irrelevant or unjust. After a while a community delineates a more or less complete picture of its idea of the good. People who strongly object to these ideas will seek to change them, or sometimes with great courage leave the community. The others are left with a comprehensive and more or less coherent concept of the good. They identify with these ideas and regard them as the ideas and norms that constitute their own behaviour and identity. They now have what we have called moral similarity and, since they all consider these norms and ideas to be constitutive ones, they tend not to feel alienated. For them, contributing to the community and its members does not mean relinquishing anything, but rather supporting what they are a part of.

New generations are then born, and are raised on more or less the same norms and values as those of the previous generation. They are involved in the cultural interaction within the community but are also open to new influences from other communities, new criticism and reflection, which comes into being whenever there is a new and different environment or new technological, economic, or cultural circumstances. This is when the debate is taken up again. By now the entire population of the community – which has become a transgenerational community – is engaged in the debate; in fact very often the debate is uninterrupted. If and when agreement is reached, some people once again discover that they are no longer able to remain in the community if their hostility to the prevailing ideas is stronger than the other connections – e.g. cultural or 'historical' – that they have with the community. For the others, a state of moral similarity has been attained once more – though perhaps only theoretically, since the common ideas and values may immediately be challenged again.

It will be useful at this point to say something about the process of rational scrutiny, or reflection, for as the reader will see later, it is an important factor in the justification of the somewhat lesser obligations that we have to very remote future generations.

There are and have been communities that have not been engaged in a reflection process. In such cases, members have a sense of obligation that supersedes any new information which might question the reasons for these obligations. Take for example a football club: if one had started to attend football matches as a supporter of Leeds United in its heyday in the early 1970s, one would probably stick to the same club forever, even though the team played in lower divisions in the 1980s. An example in the transgenerational context could be the Jewish ultra-orthodox community of Jerusalem. Scientific achievements and discoveries have not affected their basic beliefs – e.g. the belief that the world was created 5,755 years ago. In the eyes of this community, loyalty, fidelity and commitment take precedence over the existence of new facts; and if a member leaves the community – for instance, by marrying an 'outsider' – the community will practise seven days of mourning as if that person had died.

Thus, reflection does not constitute a necessary part of what every community is analytically or in the anthropological sense. As we have just seen, some solidly-established communities are traditional and reject critical reflection, or claim that reflection will always result in membership of that particular community (or else one has the wrong approach). My argument, therefore, is not that all communities correspond to my description, but rather that this represents the *normative* requirement, a certain understanding of community, and indeed the only interpretation that will fit the case of rational persons who are constituted by the values of their communities.

When there is discussion and debate to guide the experience of a community, it is almost certain that there will be changes of beliefs. But in the absence of reflection, discussion, and debate, the community loses its essential character. One should recall that we have related the community to a moral system by which a person defines herself, from which her 'self' is derived. And no rational person wishes to define herself in terms of potentially false opinions and values. We have an interest, as Raz argues, in holding valid beliefs, i.e. 'true beliefs which are constitutive of one's moral integrity, but are nevertheless subject to modifications and approving judgement' (Raz 1986: 310). Thus, reflection is a precondition for compatibility between the transgenerational community and rational behaviour.

Let me now go over the main points that were raised. It was suggested that since individualistic theories have failed to find the moral grounds for our obligations to future generations (the task of sustaining this argument has been postponed to the next chapters), it is about time to try the communitarian approach. If it is accepted that membership derives from a community and that we have obligations to other members of our community, then this implies that, if we have a transgenerational community that extends to the future, then we have obligations to future generations. The first task, then, was to demonstrate that a notion of a community with people with whom we have no daily interaction and whose identities are unclear is feasible. So the first step was to argue that daily interaction is not the phenomenon we are looking for, because it is not characteristic to communitarian relations in any case. Rather we should look for the moral and political debate and its two main components: reflection and the search for moral similarity. If, later, it could be shown that these are future-oriented, it would lead us towards an understanding of the notion of a transgenerational community that extends into the future. So, after defining the constitutive elements of the transgenerational community it is time to move on to the transgenerational community which extends into the future and to discuss our attitude to the future.

THE TRANSGENERATIONAL COMMUNITY EXTENDING INTO THE FUTURE: WHY AND HOW

The option of the fraternity model and its rejection

Why should people feel a part of the transgenerational community which extends into the future? Why should they care about the future in the first place? There are two alternative answers to these questions: one is the fraternity model, and the other is based on the notion of the rational transgenerational community.

The fraternity model explains the notion of extending a community into the future to include future generations in terms of emotions and sentiments. John Passmore, a prominent advocate of this model, argues that our concern for future generations derives from our feelings of love and care for our children: because we love our children, we care about their children, who will also be loved by our children, and so forth. Hence he regards the grounds for obligations to posterity as a 'chain of love'.

> Now, in fact, men quite often do make heroic sacrifices. They make them out of love. It is as lovers that they make sacrifices for the future more extensively than any Benthamite calculus would admit to be rational.. . . There is, then, no novelty in a concern for posterity, when posterity is thought of not abstractly – as the 'future of mankind' – but as a world inhabited by individuals we love or feel a special interest in.
>
> (Passmore 1974: 87–90)

But, unfortunately, the theory can be shown not to work. In the first place, it is wrong to base obligations on emotions – sentiments or love – alone. If we nevertheless do so, and base obligations within a single generation on love, it is a very different thing to base obligations to future generations on that principle.

Even within a single generation, obligations to a large group of people cannot be based on love alone. If it were adequate, love would lose its meaning as an *exclusive* emotion. Love is a superior relationship with a particular person, or persons, for whom one has special, exceptional feelings, above and beyond one's feelings for everyone else. Love, then, is based on particularity, whereas our relationship with future generations is one involving non-particularity or 'facelessness and impersonality' (Care 1982).

Of course we can love our immediate successors. Passmore, however, concludes that because our immediate successors will love their immediate successors, we should love, or at least care for, the latter. I disagree not so much with this specific moral demand as with the reasoning behind it. Passmore seems to argue that whatever is loved by the object of my love should also be loved by me. In other words, if I love my mother and my partner loves me, then my partner should love her 'mother-in-law'. Well, this may be true in my personal experience; nevertheless, I am sure that the experience of many readers will be different.

Consider the following: suppose that Jim loves Ruth, but she, unfortunately, loves Jack. According to Passmore, Jim should then love Jack. But the truth is that unless Jim is a super-altruist, he is liable to dislike Jack, and is unlikely to be concerned with his welfare – and not, may I say, without good reason. We see, then, that love is not contagious, and the same can be said of many other emotions. The implication for the transgenerational context is that if we love our children, we look after them. This, however, is not sufficient justification for feeling obligations to people who will live three, six or ten generations from now.

Finally, empathy with specific persons will not lead us anywhere in the multigenerational context. How can one have empathy with people one will never know? In contrast, empathy with a community – let us say, an ideological movement – does indeed make sense in this context, yet even this will not be enough, because sentiments are not sufficient for the creation of a *constitutive* community. This has been clearly demonstrated by Sandel, when he distinguished between the constitutive and sentimental conceptions of a community. In the latter, people share the sentiments of other people in their social sphere, and are consequently unselfish in their attitude towards other persons and towards the idea of social co-operation in general. But this does not satisfy the requirements of a constitutive community, because, for a society to be a community in this sense, a 'community must be constitutive of the shared self-understandings of the particip-ants and embodied in their institutional arrangements' (Sandel 1982: 173). Such a community cannot be grounded in sentiments alone. Nor is the sentimental conception of community adequate in the case of the transgenerational community we are discussing. Indeed, the fact is not that we have feelings for future generations who belong to the same community as we do, but rather that we understand the transgenerational community and all its members, no matter when they exist, as integral to ourselves and to what constitutes our identities. This is because our moral values – not simply abstract ideas, but rather part of what we are – are derived from this transgenerational community.

To conclude, sentiments are instinctive feelings characterized by enthusiasm, excitement, inspiration, or nobility of the mind. They are defined as a 'view based on or coloured with emotion' (*The Concise Oxford Dictionary* 1976) and are related to a 'tendency to be swayed by feeling rather than reason' (Hugh 1973). We should be aware of the important role that sentiments play in every community's life – they even serve as a catalyst for social and political mobilization – and of the place of emotions in the creation of communities and in the myths that are built to support and sustain them. Nevertheless, sentiments and emotions are inadequate to explain the transgener-ational constitutive community, and in fact may even be suspect, especially if they are not controlled by reason or provoke negative reactions, such as a rejection of the stranger or the non-conformist.[11]

On the other hand, sentiments, even when positive in their results, may be too weak to serve as the moral grounds for our obligations to future generations. We know that we do have some obligations to future generations; nevertheless, the sentimental view of the community does not guarantee even basic obligations to future people. People, for example, may have had sentiments of sympathy for the struggle led by 'Solidarity' in Poland, yet they did nothing actively. In short, sentiments in themselves are not sufficient motivation for acting and expressing obligations.

The rational transgenerational community: self-transcendence and one's relationship with the future

I call the other model of the transgenerational community extending into the future 'rational' because it is a more *voluntary* model of community, based on reflection. This distinction begins with the concept of one's own identity in the context of time.

One's notion of one's identity extends into the future, including those times subsequent to one's death.[12] This assertion is based on the idea of 'self-transcendence', introduced by Ernest Partridge, not as a moral aspiration but as an empirical psychological fact or psychological need, common to all 'healthy' people. We have the need to extend ourselves to others, either directly or through institutions.

> [A]s a result of the psychodevelopmental source of the self and the fundamental dynamics of social experience, well function-ing human beings identify with, and seek to further, the well-being, preservation and endurance of communities, locations, causes, artifacts, institutions, ideals and so on, that are outside the selves and that they hope will flourish beyond their lifetimes.
>
> (Partridge 1981b: 204)

Such a person 'has the capacity to place before his consciousness events and circumstances that are detached from the immediate time and place of his moment of awareness and of his physical location' (Partridge 1981c: 255), and thus has an interest in 'states of the world' which are beyond her personal happiness. As Barry writes, when one seeks to promote the case of, say, an object one has been working on, or an ideal one has believed in, what one in fact seeks is the fulfilment of one's own desires. One is less interested in whether the fulfilment takes place during one's lifetime, than in whether it takes place at all.

> If I want something to happen, I don't merely want the satisfaction of believing that it happens; and if it happens, I have got what I want even if I never have the satisfaction of hearing about it. If it is reasonable to include in interests having certain things happen (whether one knows about them or not) while one is alive, it seems strange to draw the line at one's death.
>
> (Barry 1983a: 151–2)

At this point, it is interesting to note that the scholars who discuss 'self-transcendence' regard it as purely psychological and not even a moral demand. This, surely, is what Partridge means when he asserts that a person who lacks this ability is to be pitied rather than condemned (Partridge 1981b). I accept this, and yet the reason we care, and should care, about the fulfilment of our ideas and desires even if it happens after we are dead is more complicated than has been suggested. We have a psychological motivation to do so, and in order to demonstrate this I shall put forward two claims: first, that it is plausible to speak of a 'unity of the self' over time, and second, that although this unity can be ended by death, yet, to some degree humans have found a way to overcome it. So, first a few words on the unity of the self.[13]

The 'unity of the self' implies that all the experiences, thoughts, expectations, and memories that a person has in her lifetime are related to the same person. Moreover, one's experiences are not only 'one's own', but also a part of what this person is. One cannot be a self independently of and detached from one's interests and ends. This concept is based on the distinction between 'mine' and 'me'. Thus, interests, goals, aims, and intentions are all – albeit not always – part of 'me' and not merely 'mine' (Sandel 1982: 55). Thus, we have a linkage between these desires, thoughts, and the person or 'self'. But what does it mean for different experiences to have this in common? What does it mean for a person and his desires in 1954 to be the same person with different desires in 1994?

The answer is provided by the theory of the continuity of the selves during one's lifetime. The theory is that future selves relate to one's present and past selves through the intentions, desires, etc. of the present self. This is the unity theory, according to the interpretation put forward by Jennifer Whiting (1986).[14] According to this theory there are various processes by which the identity and unity of the self are achieved. All of these, however, entail relating the self to experiences and ideas (including philosophies, ideologies, and theories) and to intentions (commitment to ideas, jobs, and roles). In other words, they involve relating the self to past and future selves.

Now, what makes the future selves of a person A part of person A is the very fact that these experiences are in certain ways related to the present experiences and intentions of that person. It is this relationship (e.g. as exemplified in the fulfilment of present intentions in future experiences) that makes the future selves a part of the person, and not the fact that both present and future experiences belong to an identical subject such as an immaterial soul. The reason I care about the future is not that there are many future selves and some of them will belong to the same organism as my present self, but rather it is the relationship between my future selves and my present self that causes me to care about the future. A similar distinction, made by Parfit, exists between 'connectedness' and 'continuity': 'If, say, I cannot now remember some earlier day, there are no connections of memory between me now and myself that day. But there may be continuity of memory. This there is if, on every day between, I remembered the previous day' (Parfit 1973: 139). So even if my future experience does not directly fulfil my past intentions, it may nevertheless relate to my past intentions if it fulfils my present intentions, which are a result of a present experience which fulfils my past intentions.

The idea of the 'unity in the self' is also proposed by MacIntyre (1981: ch. 15). For him, the continuity of the self is 'given'. Indeed, he argues, a 'narrative' view of ourselves is the only correct methodological approach to the study of actions. The narrative is like a life-story told by the person itself. Now, this life-story has a 'telos': i.e. intentions, goals, aims. Hence one's identity is a function, among other things, of one's aims. Thus all changes in the actions of a person in the course of time will be incomprehensible if detached from the setting within which they take place, i.e. the narrative. 'There is no present' says MacIntyre, 'which is not informed by some image of some future, and an image of the future which always presents itself in the form of a telos' (1981: 215). If, for instance, I am asked 'what is it that you are doing?', I can give several answers, all of which will be true. Thus, I am writing a book; I am trying to impress the publisher; I am working for payment; I am trying to satisfy my mother; I am improving my writing skills.

Now, all these answers are not only true, but are also related to each other; the thread that connects them is time. The first one – 'I am writing a book' – describes the action as it appears now, in the present. So does the third one – 'I am working for payment'. But the second – 'I am trying to impress my publisher' – and the third describe my intentions and their consequences: they relate to the future. The fourth – 'I am trying to satisfy my mother' – and the fifth – 'I am improving my writing skills' – describe unintended future consequences of my action or my present intentions which relate to both the future and the past: 'I have always known that my mother would like me to write a book', or 'My writing skills were worse before I started writing this book'. Actions, then, are inseparably related to motives, wills, intentions, concerns. In recognizing this, we can now see our lives as a long continuity, as a network of intentions and actions which are correlated and which reflect our wish to continue the self beyond temporal – as well as physical – boundaries. Thus my writing this book is not a fragmentary action, alienated from other actions, but rather one which takes place within the framework of a long period of life; not merely the short period of weeks or months in which I write the book, but rather the more distant past and future, the previous intentions and their future implementations.

But is this continuity doomed to cease when one dies? Let us return for a moment to the definition of continuity. It stands for the relations between my future selves and my present self, in that the future represents the implementation of present (or past) intentions. But if so, there is no reason why, when the body stops functioning, further future events should not count as implementations of present intentions.

This is not confirmation of personal identity after death; and yet, a part of one's personal identity during one's life is the expectation of the fate of one's acts and ideas after one's death. Indeed, we are aware of death and of the fact that it arrests continuity, and hence we fear death. However, as Nagel argues, what we fear in death is not death itself but rather the loss of life, for we do not know what death actually is, we can never know what it is to feel dead; and even if we could, we would not be able to describe it in a language that usually refers to life.

It is alleged that the failure to realize that this task [imagining being dead – A.d.S] is logically impossible (for the banal reason that there is nothing to imagine) leads to the conviction that death is a mysterious and therefore terrifying prospective state. But this diagnosis is evidently false, for it is just as impossible to imagine being totally unconscious as to imagine being dead.

(Nagel 1981: 3)

Now, what is it that bothers us about the loss of life? That it denotes either the end of our physical being or the end of our mental existence. Which one can it be? The answer brings us back to our attitude towards life. We enjoy and appreciate life, and what we appreciate about it most is not physical, but spiritual, existence. To illustrate this, think of life in a comatose state: one is physically alive, but does not possess the spiritual functions of a human being, the working of the mind. One can hardly describe continuous and endless life in a comatose condition as interesting, enjoyable, or valid at all. In fact, some people argue that in cases of a long-term coma, when there is no chance of recovering, letting the person die is the most humane and moral course of action. This indicates that we do not appreciate bodily existence *per se*. Rather it is mental activity that we value most, and thus it is the end of our mental existence that troubles us. More precisely, we are afraid of the situation described by Chekhov in his *Three Sisters*:

Yes, they'll forget us. Such is our fate. There's nothing we can do about it. The things that seem great, significant, and very important to us now will no more seem to be important with time.[15]

But, if this is the case, there is a way to overcome this fear. We can, to a certain extent, and should immortalize the creative part of us. True, this is not a total victory over the fear, nor is it a full answer. Nevertheless, if we follow this course of action, it will provide us with a certain victory.

The idea of immortalizing our present existence is not so very far-fetched. The most common way is to take photographs – 'freezing' moments of happiness, beauty, aspiration, action, importance – in short, a moment of significance. Such immortalization allows us, the living, to recall the dead. Consider the practice of hanging photographs of our deceased friends or relatives in our homes, or think of hanging photographs and erecting statues of former leaders in public buildings, or of long-dead scholars in scientific institutions, and so forth. All these denote a will to overcome the barriers of death and the interruption it causes.[16]

Now the creative self, that 'continues' after one's death, so to speak, and that reflects the notion of continuity discussed above, can provide another form of immortalization. Consider, for example, how many diaries, books of poems, collections of letters, etc. have been published posthumously, 'in memory of ...'. This is our attempt to leave to future generations the achievements of our creative self, thereby ensuring that a part of this self will still exist in the future. One's body can be buried, burned, or disposed of by whatever means; one acknowledges that there is no other way to end one's physical existence. But one's thoughts and ideas can still exist beyond physical annihilation, and in this way some part of the fear of death is overcome.

In this sense, there is no reason to think of death as the point where our future selves cease to exist: if the notion of continuity is based on the fact that our future selves respond to our present selves' intentions and desires, then posthumous situations, which respond to our intentions and desires, can be considered as some kind of continuity as well. In short, I find it very difficult to see a precise reason why the fulfilment of one's desires and intentions should stop when one dies.

Now this, I should stress, is a psychological rather than a meta-physical argument. Plato, as against this, thought that all nature seeks to be immortal and that this is attained by generation, by leaving behind a new existence in place of the old one. Plato thought that this law of succession meant that 'all mortal things are preserved, not absolutely the same, but by substitution, the old worn-out mortality leaving another new and similar existence behind – unlike the divine, which is always the same and not another'.[17] This metaphysical problem is discussed by Heyd:

> What is the value of value? If indeed all value is person-affecting, then the very existence of (affected) persons cannot ... have any value. Axiology and ethics start playing a role only on the assumption that there *are* human beings. This points to the limits of ethics.
>
> (Heyd 1992: 211, emphasis in original)

So generation is an attempt to confer meaning and value on our own existence through what Heyd calls a 'metaphysical ascent'. But then, the satisfaction of our wishes in the future is dependent on the actual existence of a future world or, more precisely, on the existence of future persons. Hence procreation is the act of giving value to value, or of creating the very conditions for value to be possible (assuming person-regarding morality). The fact of having wishes for the future is meaningless if we are not certain that future persons will actually exist (and this is something of which we can never be certain).

So this is *not* my line of argument. I am not advancing any metaphysical claim, but rather a psychological one. I do not therefore think that the means of immortalizing oneself must be through generation, the conception of children, but rather through conceiving thoughts and ideas. Similarly, I do not wish to take part in the debate on whether or not the existence of human beings is good. However, I argue that, as a psychological fact, most of us fear the loss of life, and that the end of one's own ideas, norms, and values the moment one passes on is perceived by most of us as a tragic possibility which we wish to prevent.

But then, not only the future selves of one's own lifetime are part of oneself, but the future in general can also be regarded as part of oneself, provided that events in the future reflect one's desires and intentions, inasmuch as now, in the present, one knows, wishes, or hopes they will occur, and inasmuch as one's future narrative meets and joins with others' future narratives. This future is also the future of one's ideas – the very ideas which are not merely 'one's own' but also part of what and who one *is*. This is what we mean when we say that a person orients herself – her 'self' – towards the future. We are creatures who are capable of caring about and feeling concern for the future; this is one of our basic characteristics as human beings, and this is part of what defines our personal identities. By this we can enlarge our conception of our 'self', our identities: we include in it the future of objects – human and non-human – that are part of us. And by this we mitigate – at least to some extent – our fear of mortality, of death.

THE TRANSGENERATIONAL COMMUNITY: CULTURAL INTERACTION AND MORAL SIMILARITY WITH FUTURE GENERATIONS

Our argument concerning the self and the future shows why we have a strong motivation to consider events that will take place in the remote future, and therefore to think of the future as part of what constitutes one's self. But this is not enough to justify obligations to future generations. Moreover, it does not help us in solving the question of the correct balance between obligations to contemporaries and obligations to future generations. In order to move closer to an answer, let us now leave the area of psychology and return to the moral and political sphere, engaging in a discussion of the community's inclusion of *future* people and of membership in the transgenerational community.

Let us first examine the case of a transgenerational community. The modern Israeli nation is a community formed and shaped during the last hundred years, since the early days of the Zionist movement.[18] In its early days this movement included a variety of political currents, of which the dominant one, the Socialist–Zionist, was, as its name implied, a combination of socialism and Zionism. Some of the new settlers in what was then Palestine advocated more a radical international socialism; others laid stress on nationalism or free market values.

The debate flourished; indeed, during the years between the two World Wars, many left Palestine and returned to the USSR because the social ideas of the community that was being formed were not radical enough, and they feared that the Israeli community would 'miss the future' which belonged – they maintained – to communism. Others returned to Germany or emigrated to America because they could not abide socialist and collectivist ideas. By the early 1940s, a more or less moderate Socialist–Zionist community had emerged, and the moral similarity was so strong – people had such a strong sense of community – that only very rarely were doubts raised about the settlers' commitment to serve in the military defence forces. Well before 15 May 1948, when the state of Israel was founded and laws enforcing mobilization were enacted, a great number of Jews had joined the Jewish defence forces. One per cent of the population of the young Israeli community was killed in the 1948 War of Independence, and yet the sense of obligation to fight for the community was deeply rooted in a community united in its ideas and values.[19]

The first breaches appeared in the 1960s. A new generation, no longer closely connected to Eastern Europe and subject to influences of American society, began to reflect on these ideas. Reflections on the economic system and its relevance to possible future conditions and the emerging post-industrial world persuaded many people to change their ideas about socialism and collectivism. Once again the debate flourished, not only politically but culturally as well. Eastern European collective norms gave way to the individualistic norms of market societies. American films displaced Russian literature. Folk dances became less 'relevant' and modern ballroom – eventually disco – dancing, heretofore virtually boycotted because of the 'bourgeois' values it represented, became popular. Those dissatisfied with these developments because they were too moderate emigrated to the United States, initiating a wave of emigration that has intensified since then. For many other Israelis, however, these changes bordered on the immoral, and especially after the war of 1967 and the occupation of Arab territories, those who still considered themselves socialists found themselves increasingly alienated.

The debate, again of a comprehensive cultural as well as political nature, continued into the 1970s. Two clear camps emerged, with one side advocating universal, tolerant, Social-Democratic and European values, and the other promoting ultra-nationalistic, sometimes orthodox religious and traditional values, combined with the 'American dream' of a completely free market. The controversy embraced all spheres of social life, including popular music, where a debate arose about whether future authentic Israeli music should be European oriented at all. In the late 1970s those who doubted socialism began to gain a political majority until eventually, in the elections of 1977, the right-wing parties succeeded in forming a government for the first time. Currently the community of Israel possesses a moral similarity different from the one it had forty years ago. Some concluded that they could no longer bear it and that there was nothing in common between contemporary norms and the values and dreams of the founding fathers of Israeli society; they left, or at least legitimized the act of leaving, which had been called in Hebrew *Yerida* – stepping down – rather than emigration. Yet others believe that they still have sufficient in common with all Israelis; their notion of moral similarity is presumably more flexible.

However, it is clear that moral similarity in Israel today is weak compared with the situation forty years ago. Many people so deeply disagree with the prevailing norms that they assert that they have no obligation to obey the law with respect to military service in the occupied territories. These include a growing number of youngsters, running into the hundreds, who refuse to serve there and prefer jail to co-operation with the military authorities outside the 1967 borders.[20]

The Israeli example not only illustrates how over a period of time cultural interaction can grow into moral similarity, but also how the opposite occurs: how moral similarity is weakened. In both cases, we see that there is a rational process of criticizing and evaluating the norms and ideas of the community. Hence I argued earlier that community, when distinct from cultural interaction and moral similarity, may be a somewhat 'primitive' form of relationship, inasmuch as it is merely *instinctive* and indicates an instinctive feeling of belonging and membership. Moral similarity, however, is a relationship on a higher level, because it is *rational* and follows *reflection*. It involves belonging to a *constitutive* community because it is a form of belonging that involves choice. Instinctive community can be constitutive as well, but only in the first or lower stage of community.

Now the extension of cultural interaction into the future is a logical implication both of cultural interaction with the past and of a normative demand for a state of genuine and positive cultural interaction, and hence for a genuine transgenerational community. The implication of cultural interaction with the past for interactions with the future is quite simple: just as we have cultural interaction with past generations, so – we may assume – will future generations have such interactions with us. Here one may say that the interaction is one directional, from future people to us; but what about inter-action in the other direction, from us to them? The answer is that we fulfil our role in the interaction with future people in a number of ways we discussed earlier, and especially by means of our creativity. We can take science as a major example: what is pure mathematics today may become applied mathematics within a few generations, and several inventions currently in use will still be useful in a generation or more. But the same principle applies to the humanities and the arts: a branch of historical research, for instance, may start now with a speculative assumption which will be checked only years later; the music of the contemporary composer Sir Michael Tippett is very likely to be studied and analysed with enthusiasm by music students in the future, who will benefit from it with respect to knowledge, skills and development of the imagination. Hence one can say that there is cultural interaction between Michael Tippett and the musicians of tomorrow.

Furthermore, cultural interaction has two stages. When the first has taken place, with the intention that the second should follow, then there is already a cultural interaction. An analogy could be writing a letter to a friend who has gone on a dangerous journey. I do not know when, or even if, I shall ever hear from him again. If I do get an answer, then there is undoubtedly an interaction; but isn't it also true if my letter is sent with the intention of getting an answer (and the intention that he should read it)? Similarly, in the case of intergenerational cultural interaction, one can say that the answer of future generations is expected to come, but in the remote future. So we may claim that there is cultural interaction even though mutual communication does not occur at one and the same time: this is a process of communication in steps or stages. Superficially, the interaction seems to be limited: we contemporaries can speak, they can answer, but we cannot respond to their answer. But in fact this communication will continue with the response of yet further future generations to the future generations with whom we communicate.

We have already seen that this debate includes several generations at one and the same time. But it should be emphasized that the debate is likely to extend not only over a few overlapping generations who share a common life; it will involve many generations, just as we may argue now about ideas that were originally discussed a dozen decades ago. For example, in the late nineteenth century, Westerners admired and reflected on the arts and values of ancient Greece.[21] Indeed, the reason for our study of the political philosophy of the Sophists, Plato and Aristotle, Aquinas, Kant, or Mill, is not merely to understand the history of their times, but also to consider their ideas and to see whether we have anything to learn from them, and perhaps even to adopt some of them.[22] We therefore have good reason to believe that in the same way, in five, six, or maybe more generations from now, people will debate, discuss, and weigh up our ideas, norms, and values and reflect on our art, science, education, judicial systems, economics, politics, and so forth. Thus a

> [L]iving tradition then is an historically extended, socially embodied argument, and an argument precisely in part about the goods which constitute that tradition. Within a tradition the pursuit of goods extends through generations, sometimes through many generations.
>
> (MacIntyre 1981: 222)

Such are our conclusions concerning the implication of cultural interaction with the past for cultural interaction with the future, arrived at by means of an empirical, behavioural argument. I wish to strengthen this line of reasoning further with a normative argument that the only valid process of cultural interaction is the one that extends into the future.

If and when the active debate ceases and fails to continue, the transgenerational community will lose its claim to be constitutive. In fact, can such a debate be conceived in any other way? Can the process of deliberation cease and at the same time remain a component of a *constitutive* community?

Let us see again how this debate is characterized. This is quite a simple matter, because the idea of deliberation is widespread among communitarian writers: David Miller's community members are active in the process of shaping the ideas of their community (Miller 1989: ch. 9); Michael Walzer is very sensitive to questions of public activity versus free time (Walzer 1970b); and MacIntyre writes:

> [W]hen an institution – a university, say, or a farm, or a hospital – is the bearer of a tradition of practice or practices, its common life will be partly, but in a centrally important way, constituted by a continuous argument as to what a university is and ought to be or what good farming is or what good medicine is. Traditions, when vital, embody continuities of conflict.
>
> (MacIntyre 1981: 222)

A person's moral starting-point, MacIntyre says, is inherited from the past of one's family, city, tribe, nation; or, we may add, community. These include 'a variety of debts, inheritances, rightful expectations and obligations'. Nevertheless this does not mean that one cannot, in MacIntyre's words, 'move forward', or reflect.

> Notice also that the fact that the self has to find its moral identity in and through its membership in communities such as those of the family, the neighbourhood, the city and the tribe does not entail that the self has to accept the moral limitations of the particularity of those forms of community. Without those moral particularities to begin from there would never be anywhere to begin; but it is in moving forward from such particularity that the search for the good, for the universal, consists.
>
> (MacIntyre 1981: 221)

Of course a debate so characterized, a debate such as we are talking about, cannot pause or cease: there is no final definite answer to the question of the good. By this I am not claiming that there is no single truth, nor am I contending that philosophy can never reach such a truth. Rather, I am claiming something far more modest: that, fortunately, people are somewhat sceptical, and perhaps should remain so, because any totalitarian monopoly on ideas of the good deserves to be rejected. The debate is therefore likely to continue – as it should – through the generations and into the future. We contemporaries do not think that history ends in our time, nor do we believe that our values, in that sense, are final. Rather, we would like future people to reflect on our values, just as we have reflected on the values of our predecessors.

Why should we like future people to reflect on our values? Don't we want moral similarity with them? Well, moral similarity is indeed a very important, if not crucial, component of the constitutive community. However, if we want the members of the community now and in the future to consider the community as a source of norms and values, then the moral similarity will and should be limited. If there are changes in technological, scientific, or economic circumstances, the transgenerational community that does not undergo a radical change at some stage or another will lose the grounds for its claim to be a constitutive community. This, again, is a normative claim, consistent with my earlier contention that the concept of a community is only compatible with rational agents, because the members ought not to define themselves according to values on which they have never reflected. Otherwise this cannot be a constitutive community.

To see this, let us look very briefly at the three stages of the development of moral similarity over time and relate them to the future as well. The first stage – moral similarity within a single generation (i.e. a 'regular' community) – is the first step beyond the most 'primitive' sense of community, which is purely 'historical'. For the first one or two succeeding generations, we can assume and predict a situation of relative cultural and moral stability. The children will grow up into the culture and values of their parents' generation. Just as in the context of one generation we thought of the community as constitutive of the individual inasmuch as one derives one's self-definition from the community's public and cultural life and one is brought up on the community's norms and values, so we now locate the individual in a broader context: a set of values shared by the community for a number of generations, accompanied by an active and lively debate on these values. Thus, the children will see their 'selves' as deriving from the debate on values and norms between themselves and their parents, and between themselves and even later generations. This is the second stage.

In the third stage, reflection is once again practised, but while we can assume that no drastic conclusions will be reached in the first generations, there is reason to predict a moderate change in the values of the following generations, and more radical change later on. The reasons are new circumstances, a new social environment, new technology – all of which are likely to change more drastically the further away they are from our time – as well as openness to ideas from the outside, i.e. from other communities whose ideas may infiltrate slowly but continuously into the public debate of the community (this process was illustrated by the Israeli example above).

The following seems to be a plausible description of the moral and ideological aspects of the transgenerational community in the future. When it comes about that the values of the members of the community change drastically, many members will find themselves in a state of growing alienation from the community of their ancestors. This will continue until the question arises as to whether they still regard it as the same transgenerational community, a community which defines the 'self' of its members. A time will come when it becomes questionable whether future generations will still speak of the same transgenerational community. Notice that, whereas in the first instance, I considered the community from the perspective of the outsider, I am now discussing it from the point of view of the insider, the member. Thus it is not reasonable to argue that an English person (an insider) regards herself today as inheriting the values of the English nation in the seventeenth century (and in this sense she does not think that such a transgenerational community exists), although historians (outsiders) would describe the nation both then and now by the same term, 'English', although with modifications and while noting that many changes have taken place in this nation.

We know of many people who left their communities because they no longer felt any sense of belonging, either because of changes in the ideas and norms of other members of the community, or because of changes in their own beliefs which were not accepted, or were even rejected by other members. Jesus is probably the most famous of these 'rebels'; perhaps Abraham was one as well. But consider also the 'Pilgrim Fathers', the first English emigrants to America, and their attitude to their native land, as well as the attitude of many liberals in South Africa to the norms of other whites in South Africa. Or think of the Indians in southern Mexico who abandoned their Catholicism for the message of evangelism in the late 1980s, or the Germans who emigrated from Nazi Germany – among them the members of the 'Frankfurt school' – because of their rejection of the Nazi ideology.

Abraham and Jesus exemplify the more common situation of a community continuing to maintain its values while an individual wishes to change them. In such a case, the person probably will (and ought to) leave the community if she fails to convince the others. However, we *expect* all future people to reflect on our ideas if they regard the community as a constitutive entity for their 'selves'. Reflection, then, must extend over generations into the future.

But not only will future generations reflect on our ideas, as we do and should reflect on those of past generations. In addition we contemporaries engage in future-oriented reflection. We undoubtedly want future generations to reflect on our ideas and form a rational constitutive community. But we would also like them to think that our ideas and norms have been good; so we weigh our ideas with an eye to some scenario of the future, speculative though it may be. We reflect on whether the values we hold will be adequate in the technological, scientific, and social conditions of a future society (those that we can actually predict). Science fiction is perhaps the most popular mode of such reflection, but architects, scientists, philosophers, and politicians also engage in such practices. Here I would like to provide two interesting and different examples. First, the philosopher Jeremy Bentham wrote, in an almost prophetic spirit:

> The day may come when the rest of the animal creation may acquire those rights which never could have been withholden from them but by the hand of tyranny. The French had already discovered that the blackness of the skin is no reason why a human being should be abandoned without redress to the caprice of a tormentor. It may come one day to be recognized, that the number of legs, the villosity of the skin, or the termination of the *os sacrum*, are reasons equally insufficient for abandoning a sensitive being to the same fate.
>
> (Bentham 1948 (1780): ch. xvii, section iv, note)

Second, towards the end of his well-known book on German society and its values in the past and after the Second World War, the German sociologist and politician Sir Ralph Dahrendorf (currently living in England) reflected on the question of the reunification of the two Germanies. He wrote:

> [A]lthough it is an indication that, even if the immediate

political obstacles and those economic and social ones that are accessible to political decision are cleared away, a mountain of less easily manipulable difficulties, which consist of social forces, would remain. The pivot of our analysis here is the question of democracy in Germany. What new answer to this question would a reunified Germany give? Here speculation has free play. It must be taken with all caution therefore if I derive from our analysis the conclusion that in a reunified Germany too, if she were free to decide on her constitution, the chances of democracy would be greater than in the German past. The basis of this hope is the completed revolution of modernity. . . . For the Federal Republic . . . even the much-cited reunification in peace and freedom would involve certain dangers. The clash of planned publicness and new privacy, a tradition of rigid elite organization and the cartel of anxiety, of conflicts without decision and decisions without conflict, may have many consequences that weigh the balance in one or another direction of modernity. . . . For the friend of the constitution of liberty this would create more problems than it would solve.

(Dahrendorf 1969: 425–6)

Here reflection moves in two directions. One is oriented backwards, towards the past, and the other is oriented towards the future. Thus, the continuity of reflection over time takes the following form. We contemporaries reflect on a value, or a set of values. We consider and discuss it both as an idea conceived by a past generation and as a value for ourselves or our society. If we still accept it, we then try to estimate its validity for a future society, the degree to which it suits the changes I have mentioned, and sometimes we even reject it on the grounds that it does not seem to fit the future ('This is no way to approach the twenty-first century' is quite a common manner of dismissing old-fashioned ideas). Our children will then engage in a discourse on the same value or set of values, and will be involved in the same process: i.e. with orientation towards the past, present, and future. Their children will follow the same practice in relation to this value or set of values. Eventually, some generation may decide that this value is no longer relevant or desirable. The moral similarity will then decrease. When substantive debate between the advocates of our values and those holding competing views or values is no longer genuinely possible, we will no longer be able to speak of a transgenerational community as we have defined it.

So we have seen that cultural interaction not only extends into the past but into the future as well, and that moral similarity will extend into the future, although not unrestrictedly. After some time it will lessen: that is to say, not by way of definition, but because of the empirical factors that I have mentioned and as a normative requirement of a genuine transgenerational community. We can reasonably predict that changes in technology, together with other factors, will lead to changes in the values held by future people. What is more, we would like this to happen, or at least to know that reflection will take place and that if future generations agree with our norms, values, and policies, it is because they find them good and not because they have not reflected on them. Ultimately, we would rather be sure that our transgenerational community is a genuine constitutive community than see our values forever accepted without a reasoning process taking place. At the same time, the transgenerational community based on or derived from cultural interaction and moral similarity is the institutional and moral reflection of the psychological concept of self-transcendence, as described above.

2

APPLICATIONS OF
THE THEORY

Nature's first green is gold
Her hardest due to hold.
Her early leaf's a flower;
But only so an hour.
Then leaf subsides to leaf.
So Eden sank to grief,
So dawn goes down to day.
Nothing gold can stay.

Robert Frost 'Nothing Gold Can Stay'

Obligations to contemporaries versus obligations to future generations: The principle of fading away of obligations

It is quite commonly agreed that all political communities 'either provide or try to provide, or claim to provide, for the needs of their members' (Walzer 1985: 68). But at this point we face a dilemma: we have argued for the existence of a transgenerational community, and have indicated that this elicits obligations to future members of one's community. On the other hand one also has obligations to the contemporary members of one's community, especially the worst-off. For example, we should perhaps provide cheap energy for contemporaries, yet refrain from damaging the ozone layer out of respect for future generations. How should we handle these conflicting obligations?

Utilitarian theorists, particularly economists, have tried to find the correct balance[1] by introducing a controversial method – the method of discounting the future, which will be considered in Chapter 3. However, the communitarian theory of intergenerational justice comes closer to finding the balance without recourse to this

51

controversial device. I have already argued that the transgenerational community is no less important than the 'contemporary' community and in that sense effects on future persons cannot be discounted. But one aspect of the transgenerational community as it has been described may trouble the reader, and that is the impression that it has no precise limits. Do we include six generations in this trans-generational community? Or perhaps eight? Or thirty? Or six hundred? In other words, to what extent are we to consider future generations when doing so is contradictory to the needs or demands of contemporaries?

Before answering the question, let us look at an analogous situation. One can belong at one and the same time to the Labour Party, to the Scottish nation and to an environmental group. One then belongs to several communities (to some of them in a loose sense) at one and the same time. So how should one decide between conflicting obligations to two or more of these communities? Or what is this 'art of life' (Gibbard 1989: 187) according to which we develop a loose community with regard to some topics and a closer or more intense community with regard to others?

All else being equal (i.e. if the sacrifices each obligation requires more or less correspond to the extent to which the community is in need), the answer must depend on the intensity of relations in the community, the criteria for intensity being personal and emotional ties together with moral similarity. The more intense the relations are, the stronger the obligations the community imposes. Now, emotional and personal ties represent the 'historical' sense of belonging to a community. This is an important element in itself but, as we have seen, cannot always serve as a basis for taking decisions in cases of conflicting obligations. They can do so in private decisions; then one can ask oneself, for instance, whether one would have more guilt feelings towards one's friends if one favoured A rather than B than if one favoured B rather than A. Nevertheless, most of us feel that reaching decisions in the public domain requires a consideration of a greater variety of factors. The most common of these factors is moral sympathy (see below). In other words, if we have only z units of goods to distribute and two communities are equally in need of the z units, most of us would rather see more of these goods distributed to the community with which we share norms and values.

At this point, a distinction should be drawn between this argument and a different one: specifically, that even if the amount of goods to be distributed is large, aid should be withheld from those needy communities whose ideologies conflict with our own. Of course this argument must be rejected: in such cases moral similarity is simply irrelevant. I argue that most people would rather provide for their own community if in need ('their' being defined in terms of moral similarity) than for a community with which they share nothing. But that does not mean that in cases when moral similarity is lacking we should never consider the provision of goods for the needy, nor does it imply that moral similarity is a condition for their provision (I shall expand on this when I discuss obligations to very remote future generations).

Thus, if one is not entirely certain about one's identification with the ideas of the Labour Party, but the values and traditions of the Scottish nation strike a more responsive chord, one might consider resisting Labour's decision in favour of paying the 'poll tax' in Scotland and interpret one's obligations to Scottish nationality as a refusal to pay that tax. And if one realizes that one's moral relationship to a certain environmental group is stronger, one will be less reluctant to disobey the law by participating in the group's anti-nuclear testing violent activities.

Doubting and questioning certain beliefs of the community may be a sign of a lessened *subjective* sense of community. But it is also plausible to speak of a lesser degree of community sentiments in the *objective* sense of the term. In that sense, we, as observers, notice a lesser degree of community sentiments when relations between the members – and hence the obligations they have towards each other – are weak, loose and sometimes variable, and when commitments to the community are no longer common. This can come about *inter alia* because of a lack of shared beliefs, norms, and so forth, as it does before a single community splits into two groups or more. Consider, for example, the many moral (as well as personal) disagreements in the British Labour Party before the emergence of the SDP or the Militants ('Real Labour'), or think of the growing religious tensions in the Indian sub continent before this huge area split into Muslim Pakistan and mainly Hindu India. Or think of the ideological and philosophical differences that were revealed in the German Green party before it split into two movements, the Fundis and the Realos, and in the French Greens before the formation of Génération Ecologie (cf. Prendiville 1992).

As for the transgenerational community, changes are very likely, and, in fact, they ought to occur. The community is a genuine community as long as it constitutes the identities of the members, and only as long as it does this. Now, it is this condition that determines the limits of the community, and it can relate to a territory (one's village, city, state), to an institution (one's party, kibbutz, university, class), but also to the time factor. As long as the set of ideas exists around which the community is built or organized and which is acknowledged as constituting one's 'self', one has a commitment to the community; the commitment merely reflects one's willingness to sustain this idea and the community which is built around it. But once the community adopts ideas with which one is deeply dissatisfied, one's commitment to the community becomes questionable, and with it one's affiliation to the community.

At this point, the reader may raise the following objection: 'I know that people in the future will hold different values from those I believe in now; nevertheless, if I were to live in the future, I too might hold different values'. At first glance this implies that one should not necessarily find it difficult to identify with a future community because of differences in norms and values. But one has to be careful here, because this argument is an expression of empathy rather than moral agreement. This person asserts that at the present time he is able to understand the reason for the values held by remote future generations. He does not say that at the present time he *agrees* with these values. The same applies to historical research: Quentin Skinner may claim that he can comprehend the rationale for burning witches in the Middle Ages, but he would not accept this practice now. Moreover, although we can comprehend the rationale for burning witches, we do not think that these people were right in doing so! Remote future generations will presumably be able to understand the motivation for our values, but they will be critical of these values not only in relation to their situation but also in relation to our social and political environment.

So communities and traditional values fade away over time. Thus, at some time or another, a community is likely to reach a stage of diminished transgenerational community. That is why our 'positive' obligations to remote future generations fade away, although not all our obligations to them completely vanish.

Thus our obligations to future generations will exist in the following degrees:

1 To those who exist now, we have wide and substantial obligations. I may even go to war for their sake; if they are in trouble, I may

take them into my home; I shall also expect my government to provide them with the goods that we believe everyone should have.

2   To those who exist in the near future, we have a very high level of obligations as well. Perhaps it is arguable that the degree is not as high as in the first category, but enough to make us pay regular taxes and so forth. For example, many believe it reasonable to be taxed for the sake of sending a spaceship into space, although only those who will live three or even seven generations from now will benefit from this research or use the spaceship regularly. The people of several picturesque old cities in Italy have decided not to allow cars into the city centre, not only because of health problems for contemporary inhabitants, but also because the pollution damages the beautiful and historically significant monuments. So it is in the category of decisions made for the sake of future generations, although contemporaries do not necessarily benefit from these decisions.

3   Towards remote future generations we have weaker obligations. I may agree to be temporarily taxed to provide a certain relief for these people (e.g. to reduce the danger of chemical pollution in their time), and I must avoid causing them any foreseeable harm even if it costs me more in terms of money or effort (and hence, for example, I may have to give up the use of nuclear energy). However, most of us will not agree to pay regular taxes to improve their welfare, *if* it lessens our support for the worse-off among contemporaries and less-remote future generations.

The crucial role of moral similarity in our relationship with future generations

We have already seen that the transgenerational community that is based on moral similarity is the moral and institutional reflection of the psychological idea of self-transcendence. I have also claimed that the emergence of a lack of moral similarity (and cultural interaction) indicates a stage in which a somewhat different community might emerge in the future. At this stage, self-transcendence as described above becomes in a certain sense irrelevant. We therefore, I have argued, have less intensive obligations towards these very remote generations. But why is it the lack of moral similarity that is all-important rather than any other factor in the transgenerational community?

The answer is that this is the most crucial element with regard to one's membership of a community, and in particular a trans-generational community, which, unlike the community within a single generation, is less likely to be related to factors such as common territory or interaction in daily life.

Let us examine this argument. The question that we must ask ourselves is, 'when will I cease being a member of my community? Under what conditions?' Let us consider these questions with regard to my personal voluntary membership of my nation.[2] Four answers are possible.

1   *I can never leave my nation. Even if I emigrate to another country, I shall remain an Israeli.*   Two difficulties arise here; the first concerns the principle of determinism and conservatism discussed earlier. The second difficulty is whether it is empirically true that one cannot leave one's community. What happens to emigrants? Can they genuinely leave their communities of origin? I am not certain, and I assume that both negative and positive answers will be controversial. Some emigrants wish to remain in their previous cultural environments, whilst others adopt the moral ideas and culture of their new political communities.

2   *I shall not be a member of my nation when everyday inter-action ceases.*   In other words, I remain part of the Israeli nation because I have always worked with Israelis and played football with them, or because I went to school in Israel. Only if this is changed (say, I won't be able to work in Israel) will I leave the nation. My answer is that if these conditions are changed – if, for instance, I cannot work with Israelis any longer – I may or may not regret it, but I would not usually care enough to describe it as leaving the nation (although I might leave the state – that is something else). A Palestinian who works and lives in Tel Aviv does not wish to join the Israeli nation, and a Turkish 'Gastarbeiter' in Germany does not necessarily, and may not wish to, leave the Turkish nation.

3   *I shall cease being a member of my nation when I can no longer agree with the main common values, norms and ideas of this community; or, that is to say, when I no longer regard these ideas as constitutive of my personal identity.*   When the community's values clearly and manifestly contradict my basic intuitions about the good, 'when the public experience of my society ceases to have any meaning for me . . . when the goals, norms or ends which define the

common practices or institutions begin to seem irrelevant or even monstrous', I shall probably try to leave the community (Taylor 1975: 381, 384).[3]

Now, compare moral similarity with everyday interaction. Imagine that I leave Israel and settle in Alaska for financial reasons or motives (which is everyday interaction). I agree with everything that is going on in Israel; I hold the same values and norms. However, I no longer interact with Israelis. People in Alaska can then rightly say, 'You are still one of them, you are like them in every respect'. But suppose I leave Israel because I can no longer bear the values, norms, ideas, and political traditions (the moral similarity) of that nation. Nevertheless, for financial reasons I have commercial relations with many Israeli companies. In that case, people around me in my new home cannot correctly say that I am still one of the Israelis, because I no longer identify with them. I do not share their moral beliefs, perhaps I even criticize Zionism, the very core of the Israeli ethos. My only relations with them are economic, but notice that we have excluded these relations from our perception of community. We saw that communitarian relations are not total or holistic, in the sense that there are spheres of life which are non-communitarian, e.g. the market. Therefore I cannot be said to remain in the Israeli community for that reason. This simply follows from the very definition of communitarian relationships.

Notice that although moral similarity is the highest level of communal association, it is not sufficient on its own to provide the basis for a transgenerational community or obligations. For instance, suppose we meet some Martians who happen to think the same way as we do about many issues, and even have the same values and norms. Let us say they are the Greens from Mars. Does this mean that we have any obligations to them? The answer is negative. Notice, however, that if these people stay on earth they will be more likely to join a Green party than a capitalist one. After some time, a cultural interaction will develop with them, and thus a sense of community will arise and obligations will be acknowledged. So moral similarity was not enough, but it is the decisive element in the community that will then emerge.

4   However, there is a fourth possibility. Suppose I leave Israel because of a lack of moral similarity just as in the second example. But somehow I cannot help myself: for better or worse, it has been my identity. So I listen to the radio broadcasts from Israel, I read

every book that is published there, purchase all Israeli records, and so forth. I criticize the ideas, values, and politics of Israel, but I keep in close touch. This points to the interesting possibility of cultural interaction despite very little, if any, moral similarity. Have I left the community in that case? I would argue that I have not.

Let me put it in this way: the most stable and substantial trans-generational community is one with more, rather than less, moral similarity. And yet we must acknowledge that this is not always the case, and may not be the case. More often we find a much lesser degree of moral similarity together with a process directed towards attaining more, as some people make an effort to alter their values while others may be indifferent and inactive. An open and genuine debate on values is therefore a crucial element in a transgenerational community. One can then remain in the community if and as long as one thinks one has a chance of persuading one's fellows of the rightness of one's way of thinking and ideas. (However, this may not be sufficient to halt the process which is very likely to occur in the generations to come, i.e. the fading-away of moral similarity.)

So, as our community progresses through time, it tends to reach a lesser and lesser degree of cohesion. Since obligations derive from relationships and a sense of community, and since these are diminished the obligations are diminished also. In this way we arrive at a 'fading-away of obligations'. From a certain stage in the future, the more remote in time future generations are, and the more the light of these moral codes and norms grows faint, the more the obligations we owe to members of the transgenerational community will be lessened. This principle implies that our obligations to not-very-remote future generations and to contemporaries should have the same weight in both their fiscal and their environmental policies: governments should consider the welfare of future generations to the same extent that they consider the welfare of contemporaries. It implies greater efforts than have hitherto been expended on the conservation of rare species, beautiful landscapes, historical monuments, the cessation of the depletion of natural resources, minimum pollution, and so on.

'But', you may ask, 'exactly how much do we have to consider future generations?' I would reply that a moral theory can assert that a government should take into consideration the welfare of future generations just as it considers the welfare of contemporaries, because these future generations form part of our transgenerational community. A right to be considered deriving from membership of our community consequently applies to future generations as well. However, the moral theory should offer principles according to which distribution should take place (i.e. concerning those to whom one should distribute). But the precise decision as to how much of what and when to allocate must, I believe, be taken politically and democratically.

Now not all distributive acts affect future generations, at least not drastically. Thus, in general, when distribution affects only contemporaries, governments should distribute to contemporaries. When distribution affects future generations, as is the case in almost all environmental policies, governments should take future generations into account in a reasonable way and to a sufficient degree. What is 'sufficient' should be determined politically, provided that all who participate in the decision are genuinely aware of the moral demands of intergenerational justice. In other words, when certain obligations to future generations contradict other obligations to contemporaries, we should not immediately favour the contemporaries rather than the future generations. Governments very often face such dilemmas of conflicting obligations. For instance, the high price of milk must sometimes be reduced because children need milk. On the other hand, the profits of dairy farms urgently need to be increased – i.e. by raising the prices of milk products. Such cases should be solved politically and democratically, and the contradictory obligations to future people and contemporaries is a case of this type, because future generations form part of our own transgenerational community.

Now, we asked what the crucial element in a transgenerational community was and how it determined the limits of our obligations to future generations. The answer to the first question is both cultural interaction and – to a major extent – moral similarity. That it is not everyday interaction is a reasonable assumption if one thinks that a community, although involved in many spheres in one's life, still leaves some room for non-communitarian relations and interactions. We saw that, in the absence of moral similarity, the community is likely to fade away and one may well ask oneself whether one should still consider it a living, constitutive community. However, a transgenerational community does not have to reach the stage of an absolute moral similarity as long as there is (a) an active debate on the idea of the good, (b) some common agreement (mainly on account of a common moral tradition) as a background, and (c) a will to reach agreement, not in the sense of attaining minimal consensus but in the sense of an openness to persuasion.

At this point the objection might be raised that the idea put forward so far of a shared moral community reflects a conception of community which is chauvinistic and relies more heavily on a distinction between 'us' and 'them, the others' than on constitutive norms and values. According to this view, individuals tend to identify with a particular community in order to find protection against the hostile or the alien. Thus, the shared values among a certain group represent nothing but the response, sometimes racist or chauvinist, of a group which rightly or wrongly imagines itself to be threatened by the norms of 'outsiders'. So I wish to dismiss this objection before I go on to discuss our obligations to remote future generations.

The above objection relates to an irrational community, whereas my discussion has so far concerned the rational stage of a community, which comes about after a critical scrutiny of the community's values in relation to values from outside the community. That is, the rational transgenerational community is a stage reached after serious consideration, accompanied by a genuine openness, has been given to so-called 'alien' values. Indeed, I have mentioned that moral similarity is possible only after 'cultural interaction', which is also meaningful and important for the existence of a transgenerational community. Cultural interaction implies a deliberation on ideas and norms, and a genuine deliberation is not one that is dominated by an irrational fear of the stranger and his or her ideas and norms. On the contrary, in the model I have presented norms and values from outside the community are perceived not as hostile but as potential new norms and values for one's own community. To see this, let us remember that communities are not necessarily national communities. For example, does the community of environmental philosophers become biocentric because they find themselves challenged by the anthropocentric philosophers? Of course not!

Perhaps it is worthwhile at this point to say a few words about the communitarian theory and toleration or liberalism in general, because the above objection has often been raised against communitarianism, without seriously taking into account the possibility that communitarianism is in general a liberal theory, although not an individualistic one.[4] It has been argued that communitarianism is either too conservative or too chauvinist when it claims that the values of the community are constitutive convictions and thus beyond the realm of reflection (Ketab 1989). My claim is twofold: first, that communitarianism is different from conservatism in that it frequently seeks to find shared interpretations, and is thus open to reflection on new ideas and to self-criticism, whereas conservatism favours the already existing and is therefore likely to sink into traditional forms and patterns without even knowing why it respects these customs beyond the mere fact that they already exist. But, second, I argue that communitarianism not only does not need to place the values of the community beyond the realm of reflection but that it cannot do so because it is implausible and makes no sense. It is irrational to claim that a value X is constitutive for you and at the same time that it is beyond the sphere of reflection because, if X is constitutive in the sense that it is good, then the value $-X$ must exist (and is wrong). This value may be constitutive for another person or group. Thus, if X is constitutive for Melissa, then $-X$ may be constitutive for Daniel.

Now if Melissa says that Daniel has therefore no right to exist or that he is somehow inferior, then Melissa is a chauvinist. If she asserts that she has X and he has $-X$ and that they therefore have nothing in common, then Melissa is a typical conservative. Moreover, in either of these cases Melissa cannot claim to be constituted by X in a rational sense because X must be regarded as conceivably false or wrong until it has been proved otherwise. But in the version of communitarianism put forward here, Melissa says: 'Well, I am constituted by my group's conviction X, and you are by $-X$; this is legitimate. Now, let us not be satisfied with declaring that this is the situation, or that we should respect each other's values. Pluralism requires that we should debate on these values. Perhaps I am wrong? Perhaps you are wrong? Wouldn't you like to examine these values as I am doing?' Moreover, our communitarian declares that even if, after the debate, she still thinks her X rather than $-X$ is good, she will remain tolerant to $-X$ and to Daniel.

There is nothing inconsistent between claiming that a value X is constitutive for Melissa and that Melissa is tolerant towards Daniel and $-X$. On the contrary: since Melissa thinks that it is important that people realize that they are constituted by the values of their communities, she is aware that there is a variety of contexts in which one is constituted, and all these contexts should flourish, if possible. In other words, the community should remain tolerant of all values and refrain from defining them as 'alien' because this pluralism is part of the process of the 'constituted self', and thus the community should encourage debate and the process of critical scrutiny.

The essence of the communitarian theory is not that Daniel is constituted by his community as against Mellisa's community, but rather the fact that Daniel and Melissa's membership of communities enriches their 'selves'. In this respect, the community of cultural interaction and moral similarity is the sphere in which shared values are debated. The process of finding the 'balance between shared values and "other values"' (Herman 1992) – of deciding which values to adopt, with which values one can coexist, and which values and norms should be rejected (e.g. pagan practices such as offering maidens' hearts to the gods) – is communitarian: i.e. it takes place within the sphere of the community.

To summarize my answer to the objection: in the model I have described, local practices, 'our' practices, are not the values of the community: they are the *sources* of the community's values. Seeing them as such, the community is ready to reflect on them by opening itself to 'other' values, and regarding the latter as potential truths rather than as something inimical. Feeling oneself to be part of a certain community does not imply that one cannot appreciate, or at least respect, the values of other communities. We can now return to the subject of posterity, and discuss our obligations to remote future generations.

OBLIGATIONS TO REMOTE FUTURE GENERATIONS

If we do not maintain communitarian relations with very remote future generations, don't we have any obligation to them? There are those who emphatically deny that we do; I would like to argue that we most certainly do. Earlier I mentioned the theory advanced by M.P. Golding, who perceives no obligations at all to very remote future generations, arguing that it would be unwise, from both the ethical and practical perspective, to seek to promote the good of the very distant (Golding 1972: 70). He leaves them in the hands of the free market, suggesting that, actually, all we have to do for very remote future generations is not plan anything for them. But while some communitarians take the position that we do not have any communitarian obligations to the remote, they still do not neglect them. For instance, Walzer writes that:

I need not take the injured stranger into my home, except briefly, and I certainly need not care for him or even associate with him for the rest of my life. My life cannot be shaped and determined by such chance encounters.

(Walzer 1985: 33)

But at the same time Walzer acknowledges that in many cases there should be some kind of compensation for the lack of communitarian obligation. For instance, Australians do not have a communitarian obligation to permit entry to emigrants from Southeast Asia; on the contrary, a radical and controversial communitarian argument is an excuse not to permit them into the community. Nevertheless, says Walzer, Australians should increase foreign aid or cede land for these people (Walzer 1985: 47–8).

This implies that we cannot simply turn a blind eye to a needy person, even if she is not in our community. It is arguable that we cannot and should not let every needy person join our community if by so doing we would violate our obligations to the needy or worse-off members of our community (assuming that there is a finite quantity of resources such as jobs etc. available). All the same, we should not be indifferent to their plight. Moreover, one might concede that we do not have an obligation to provide for the needs of every stranger (e.g. for remote future generation) but still rightly claim that we should refrain from causing severe predictable harm to any human being, no matter whether or not she belongs to our community. As already noted, many of our environmental policies, such as storing radioactive waste, are likely to harm remote future generations. This is morally wrong, and we should find a way to store nuclear waste securely or, if as many scientists argue this is impossible in the present state of our knowledge, we should either put aside huge sums of money to help future generations in their search for better and safer means of storage (which implies that nuclear energy would become very expensive, and thus rarely used) or, even better, we should abolish nuclear power entirely. In short, we do have certain obligations to remote future generations, although they are not based on, or derived from, communitarian relationships.

This is a matter of humanity rather than of justice. The difference between the two is that justice is concerned with principles of ownership or the control of resources, while humanity is concerned with people's well-being. It requires us to avoid the infliction of suffering and to relieve it where it occurs (Barry 1982).

I subscribe to the view – as I assume my readers do – that it is morally obligatory to behave humanely. Nevertheless, the demands of justice are somewhat more basic than the demands of humanity. There are different degrees of obligations: some are more pressing than others, some are more basic than others. Obligations which derive from considerations of justice are more basic than obligations that derive from humanity, although obligations that derive from humanity are sometimes more pressing. For instance, the relief of the suffering of the hungry people of Somalia is a very urgent matter, and a citizen of, say, England should therefore expect her government to do whatever it can in that direction. On the other hand, it seems to me that it would be just if the control over water in England were not in the hands of only a few. Justice requires that it should be in the hands of everyone or, in other words, of the government. This obligation of the better-off to the least advantaged in England is perhaps less pressing, but much more basic, inasmuch as it demands a redistribution of control over resources and inasmuch as it applies continuously, all the time, whereas the obligation to the people of Somalia is for a certain purpose and only until the distress is relieved.

Thus, those of our obligations to future generations which derive from justice apply in the context of our relations with the more immediate future generations, i.e. the transgenerational community, which is the context within which provision and distribution of control of and ownership of goods take place. Those of our obligations to future generations which derive from humanity, on the other hand, apply in the context of our relations with very remote future generations. This is a sphere in which we cannot distribute the control of goods.

My argument, nonetheless, is that although we have somewhat less basic obligations to remote future generations, the fact that we have such obligations indicates that obligations to *all* future people are incumbent upon us. These obligations are not a matter of charity, nor are they a matter of supererogation or generosity. Moreover, although I refer to these obligations as 'negative', I do not wish by this to imply that our obligations to human beings may be reduced to simply refraining from certain policies. Rather, it is clear that in addition to pursuing active policies we should also practice certain policies which will prevent certain situations. For example, in order to prevent hunger we should allocate considerable financial resources to agricultural and biological research for the improvement of nutrition. We should therefore accept the principle that we should sacrifice something (how much and what is a separate question) for the sake of remote future generations. At the same time, it is unreasonable to think in terms of sharing control over goods with people who will live two thousand years from now.[5]

3

THE UTILITARIAN THEORY AND THE NOT-YET-BORN

A statesman thinks of the next generation, a politician of the next election. A politician who is also a statesman arranges for the next elections to be held in the next generation.

Aharon Shemi, As a Wise Man Once Said

INTRODUCTION

Not one, but several, utilitarian theories of intergenerational justice are in existence. Each of these theories makes a simple claim: that the best policy or action is the one likely to promote most over-generational happiness or utility (satisfaction of desires, wants, preferences), and cause least overgenerational pain. In other words, the utilitarian theory of intergenerational justice refers to the balance between the pain and the happiness that is caused by an act, measured or calculated with an eye to its consequences for future generations. In this respect, utilitarianism is a form of consequentialism: the consequences of an act or a policy are the reason for approving or disapproving of that policy or act. A policy that affects future generations is judged according to its consequences in their time in addition to the way it affects us contemporaries. Now, all con-sequentialist theories approve the act which produces the 'best' state of affairs; but since there are many criteria for defining the best outcome of an act or policy, there may be several consequentialist theories. I shall therefore concentrate on the most popular among them, namely utilitarianism. So it should be noted that my criticism is directed to consequentialism in general only when I discuss the idea that people ought to maximize good and minimize evil.

The principle of the maximization of happiness or utility is sometimes supported by an argument of a psychological legitimacy, according to which what people generally want is to maximize their utilities or happiness, and their way of acting is governed by this desire. Added to this is an ethical argument that it is a good thing that people behave this way (i.e. aim at maximizing their happiness or utilities). The utilitarian presumes that we are discussing voluntary acts and that a few (or at least two) alternatives are open to the agent. For example, suppose that a policy of building a factory in a city produces hundreds of jobs for both its present and future populations, and causes minimal pain to a small community of fishermen who often go fishing in the river, now badly polluted.[1] More happiness than pain is produced, which is sufficient justification for adhering to this policy. However, if an inexpensive alternative exists whereby a canal can be dug for the chemical wastes that will thereby bypass the fishermen's village and thus enable succeeding generations of fishermen to go on fishing, a utilitarian will embrace the second policy rather than the first.

Now, it may be asked why consider future persons in the first place? Utilitarians respond that their theory is a universal ethic in that it considers each person's interests to the same degree as everyone else's, according to the formula that is often attributed to Jeremy Bentham: 'Each to count for one, no one to count for more than one.' This universalism embodies a principle of impartiality, of which utilitarians are proud. The implication is that one's race, gender, nationality, etc. are irrelevant factors in the utilitarian calculation. But just as the utilitarian is indifferent to the question of *where* one comes from, she is indifferent to the question of *when* one 'comes from', i.e. when one lives, or when the utility is realized. Happiness, or utility, is as intrinsically good this year as it will be ten, twenty or five hundred years from now (Hospers 1972: 211; Sumner 1978). This is the case, one should note, only on condition that we are certain that the happiness or the utility will truly occur, for utilitarians acknowledge that there are times when remote goods or utilities are less likely to occur, and for such cases have developed theories of discount, which I shall discuss below.

The appeal of utilitarianism in the intergenerational context lies in the following aspects. First, the utilitarian calculation considers the effects and consequences of an act or a policy, and this is precisely what many people do when they talk about intergenerational justice and future generations. They do not concentrate merely on the effects of our acts in the present, but consider their longer-term consequences as well, or how they affect the future. Even good motives (e.g. bettering the welfare of contemporaries) are pushed aside if the consequences for future generations are horrific. Therefore these people ask: why not simply adopt a consequentialist theory which already takes into account the effects of acts and policies? The only effort we have to make – it seems at first glance – is to consider some possible ramifications on the more remote future, and consider them within the already-existing framework. Second, we are constantly aware that, although we may be able to find a just intergenerational principle today, nobody can guarantee that it will be relevant in a few generations' time, so it may have to be changed to suit the change in circumstances. The utilitarian principle, however, is flexible in that it permits us to adapt our acts to changing circumstances in the future as long as we adhere to the principle of maximizing happiness or utility. Thus, the formula we choose may well be valuable for many generations (cf. Smart and Williams 1973: 64). Moreover, the utilitarian theory does not regard acts as intrinsically good or evil, and so enables us to consider a policy to be right in one set of circumstances and wrong in another. So, at first sight at least, it seems only natural and suitable to use the utilitarian approach in our discussion. Or is it?

THE UTILITARIAN THEORY AND POPULATION POLICY

In my discussion of intergenerational justice so far I have not yet given detailed consideration to topics that come under the heading of population policies. Examples of such topics are, for instance, the question of whether we have a duty to produce a certain child or to refrain from reproduction, or broader questions about the optimal size of the population. It has been argued that solutions to environmental problems are a function of population policies (Huxley 1956; Hardin 1968). In my view, these questions do not exhaust the environmental issue, and are somewhat different, although not wholly distinct, from the issue of distribution between generations. Population policies do, in fact, partly address the issue of whether we owe future generations anything, even life itself; but distribution policies address the issue of what and how much we owe them. There is undoubtedly a correlation between these issues, but this book is not the place to discuss in depth the whole matter of population policy.

All the same, utilitarian philosophers find themselves discussing these questions time and again even when their main target is the issue of intergenerational distributive justice. The reason is obvious: the utilitarian principle holds that we must follow a policy which promotes happiness or a similar factor more than any alternative policy. If this is the case, questions of population policy immediately arise: e.g. if my child is going to be happy, do I have a duty to create her and by this means increase overgenerational happiness? If my child is going to be less happy than the average, ought I to refrain from conceiving her? If we are to maximize happiness, does this mean we should produce more and more children, as long as they are happy? Another reason to consider population policy issues, at least for the total utilitarian, is that she must ultimately know the size of the population for her calculations. How can one possibly discuss the notion of total happiness without knowing the number of people? And if this is the case, then the utilitarian must determine the size of the population before she discusses questions of justice.

Now a policy of ours can affect someone who is not yet born in two ways. It can affect people's very existence, i.e. it may determine whether they are going to exist or not, and, more generally, our acts may affect the number of future generations, the size of each generation, and the identities of future people. Or a policy may affect people's lives: that is to say, their standard of living or quality of life. Thus, a distinction can be made between possible persons – those whose existence is dependent on our acts (i.e. until we have decided how to act) – and future people – those who will live after we have decided upon the policies. But the two ways in which a policy affects the not yet born are correlated, which causes particular complications.

When utilitarianism refers to a fixed population – as indeed it usually does – it maintains that we should act in such a way as to maximize the population's total or average happiness. In the case of a fixed population there is no real difference. But, when we are dealing with future people, the utilitarian is in trouble. If the utilitarian chooses the principle of average happiness, she will be confronted with the following absurdity: [2] Suppose that I live in a very happy community and think of conceiving a child who will be happy, although somewhat less happy than the average. Should I not bring him into the world? Average utilitarianism (the principle of average happiness) directs us not to conceive the child in that case, because average happiness would be reduced if we did so. This recommendation is misguided and unacceptable, because if my child, as well as my partner and myself, is going to be happy, why shouldn't the child be conceived? Usually, when we add one good (a happy child) to another good (a happy couple, family, community) we view the result as at least as good as the original state of affairs, if not better. This illustrates the problem with regard to average utilitarianism and population policies, namely, that the answer to the question of whether one should have a (certain) child or not becomes a function of an irrelevant factor, i.e. the average level of happiness in a society.

Should we reject average utilitarianism in the case of inter-generational relationships? Narveson tackles this challenge by distinguishing between the viewpoint of the impersonal bystander and that of the concerned participant, i.e. the parent. From the point of view of society, we should adopt principles which make it harder for people to have children who are unlikely to lead happy lives; but parents should be permitted the great happiness of parenthood even if their child may be slightly less happy than average (Narveson 1976: 74). But Narveson's explanation is mistaken. The fact of the parents' happiness surely implies that the average happiness will not be reduced, whereas the above case assumes that the average happiness *is* going to be reduced. In other words, the utilitarian has to make up her mind whether she takes into account the happiness of the parents as well, or only that of the newborn baby. And even if she does consider the parents' happiness, it still may be – in a very happy society – that the average happiness of this society will be reduced if the child is conceived. It is possible that Narveson himself is aware of the weakness of his solution for he offers another:

> [i]f . . . it was merely said that this [producing the child – AdS] would be less than the best thing to do, but not actually wrong, then perhaps the consequence would be less paradoxical.
>
> (Ibid.)

This admittedly interesting attempt to avoid the difficulty implies a departure from utilitarianism, however. Actually, average utilitarianism does not simply assert that conceiving the child is less than the best option, but says, rather: 'If you are undecided whether to conceive or not to conceive, then it is better not to conceive. You ought not to conceive.' This, as we have seen, is both ridiculous and outrageous.

Further, the principle of average utilitarianism can lead us towards a very cruel population policy and an undoubtedly immoral conclusion: one alternative means of increasing happiness which average utilitarianism finds difficult to dismiss or reject is the elimination of unhappy people.[3] We have seen that, if we do not add unhappy children to our society, then average happiness will increase, assuming that we add happy ones. While this sounds plausible to many, the more radical way of increasing average happiness is by decreasing the number of unhappy people in our society by getting rid of some who are miserable. Average utilitarianism may still be defended by the argument that it is indeed reasonable in some cases to talk of reducing population (e.g. when there is severe famine, it might be better if fewer people were sharing the same resources). But then, this would only be true – if it is at all – when it is impossible to maintain the level of happiness, for instance by supplying food. Average utilitarians may go even further and demand a reduction in the number of unhappy people in every case. This, of course, leads to absurdities: suppose that in a certain society there are ten people, two of whom are miserable and the rest happy. There is no hunger in this society, so none of the eight happy people would gain utility – e.g. more food – if the two unhappy people were to die. But if it were the case that only the eight happy people existed, average happiness would increase. So we discard the two miserable ones. Then it appears that among the eight there are some who are happier than others, so we should get rid of the four less happy ones, and so on and so forth. As long as eliminating the number of unhappy people does not affect the happiness of the happy ones – and unfortunately such a dreadful situation is conceivable – the calculations of average utilitarianism in cases of undetermined population sizes (such as that of future generations) direct us to adopt this policy. Is total utilitarianism better in this respect?

If we choose total utilitarianism, we face another absurdity: if we are to maximize happiness, we must maximize the number of happy people. If every child that exists is happy (assuming that it is almost always better to live than not to, so that every child has some degree of happiness), then we have to give birth to the maximum number of children. Notice that there is no need for future children to be happier than their parents; we could increase total happiness even by producing less happy children who are nevertheless happy to some degree. In that case, average happiness decreases but total happiness increases. Thus, according to total utilitarianism, we are obliged to produce as many children as possible, as long as their happiness exceeds their misery, or as long as their existence adds to the total sum of human happiness (i.e. the total happiness of the whole population, including the effect of the newly-born on those who are already alive). Even if there is disutility caused to some by adding happy children, e.g. the disutility to those who will have to share resources with the newborns, we could always consider this disutility as negligible compared with the happiness of the newborn.

It might be useful to pause here and briefly examine an idea which is pertinent to this argument, namely Parfit's notion of 'person-regarding morality': i.e. that duties must always be directed towards someone. Earlier I described the distinction between future and possible people. Now, Narveson argues that only future people count in the intergenerational context because, if we have any duties to future persons, then they are 'person-regarding'. And similarly, if an action affects no one, that action (or inaction) cannot be the violation or fulfilment of a duty (Narveson 1978: 43; Parfit 1984).

There are several interesting implications of person-regarding morality in this instance. First, it makes it impossible to talk of having a duty to preserve the human race. For if we have such a duty, it is to certain people – namely, future persons, and not to a general phenomenon such as the human race. But if we do not carry out this duty, we find ourselves with no future persons to whom this duty (or our failure to carry it out) can be directed (Narveson 1978: 43). Furthermore, the claim that we should produce a child if he is going to be happy can be rejected on the same grounds, simply because, if we do not produce him, there is no one to whom the obligation refers. Narveson introduces a modification here. One does not have a duty to reproduce unless bringing forth the child will prevent suffering (Narveson 1976: 72). In general, Narveson claims that there is no moral obligation to produce a child even if we could be sure that he will be happy throughout his life, but there is a moral obligation not to produce a miserable child. Paradoxically, this leads us to conclude that it is always better not to produce a child, for if it turns out that the child is happy, no duty is fulfilled or violated, but if he is miserable, a duty is violated if we conceive the child and fulfilled if we do not. So in both cases not producing is better (cf. Vetter 1971).

In order to avoid these complexities, a total utilitarian can defend her principle by claiming that, rather than seeking to maximize happiness, she would like to affect the happiness of a given population. Thus, we are not obliged to increase the number of happy people, but the happiness of whatever number of people there are. Or in Narveson's words, our aim is 'the greatest happiness *of* the greatest number and not ... the greatest happiness *and* the greatest number' (Narveson 1967: 63), and 'we are in favour of making people happy, but neutral about making happy people. Or rather, neutral as a public policy, regarding it as a matter for private decision' (Narveson 1976: 73).

It does appear, though, as if such a total utilitarian is, by this affirmation, stepping beyond utilitarian limits. For her solution to these paradoxes is alien to utilitarianism, making the utilitarian principle dependent on a society of a given size, a certain community of people, and asserting that it is the happiness of this community and these people that we should consider. The solution bars the entry to non-members of the society, who, not being included in this calculation, are not equally respected. But what, then, has become of the idea of universal ethics and impartiality? If the question is whether to maximize total happiness by increasing your happiness or by conceiving your happy great-grandchild, our total utilitarian would say that we should give preference to you, whereas utilitarianism – as we have seen – claims to be impartial towards temporal location, and should therefore take an impartial position between you and the great-grandchild, all other things being equal.

If this is not sufficient grounds to dismiss the utilitarian principle, Derek Parfit's depletion case presents a serious challenge to every utilitarian. Originally put forward as a provocative argument against person-regarding morality, this paradox later became the subject of a great deal of discussions, being dealt with again by Schwartz (1978), Kavka (1982), and others.[4] Parfit's argument is along these lines:

1 If a person had been conceived in a month other than that in which she actually was conceived, she would have been a different person.
2 Policies do affect people's behaviour and destinies, which implies also the identity of future persons. For example, had there not been a train strike on a specific day, my father would have not taken a bus, he would have not met my mother and hence I would not exist.
3 Suppose that we had to choose between two alternative policies. One is to deplete a high percentage of the available resources, and the other is to conserve them. The result of the former would be a much higher standard of living for the present generation. Many children would then be conceived – different children than those conceived had we chosen the other alternative – and they would

have much less in terms of resources, clean environment, and wealth than we had. The result of the latter policy would be a higher standard of living for future people, yet these would be different people from the ones who would be born as a result of the former alternative.

Now, the paradox is that if we have a policy of depletion, we do not harm anybody, for had we chosen the other policy, different persons would exist. Thus, if we choose depletion, there will be no one to come and 'blame' us. Future persons, who will have very little, will still appreciate the fact of being alive and will not consider themselves to have been harmed. In short, it is not wrong for us to decide upon a policy of depletion because it will not harm people who will live in the future. This paradox reveals that, according to utilitarianism, we really have no duty to future generations because the fact that it is they and not others who would be produced implies that they would benefit and as such have no right to complain about distribution, welfare, and so forth.

In applying Parfit's argument to our discussion on utilitarianism, two objections can be raised. One is that we should look at future society rather than at future people. It does not matter, the argument goes, that as a result of two different policies different people exist; a future *society* would exist under both policies. Whereas no individual would be better off as a result of one policy rather than another, the future society would benefit more from one of them, which is, therefore to be preferred. But this argument would be immediately dismissed by utilitarians, because according to them maximizing the utility of a society, rather than individuals, is not a valid moral reason for adopting one policy rather than another.

Another possible challenge is to argue as follows. 'We should not be concerned that under one policy certain people will exist and under another policy different people will exist. We should simply measure the amount of utility that each policy will bring to present and future people whoever they are, and decide accordingly which is the preferable policy.' 'Suppose', the argument runs, 'that you have to choose between giving two pounds you have in your pocket to a beggar in the street and using them to buy some sweets for your daughter. All you have to do is to estimate the amount of happiness that you will give each of them if you spend the money one way or the other, and then act accordingly.' Therefore the right utilitarian formula in the case of depletion is the one which says that, since we ought to do what would benefit people most, it would be worse if *those who live* are worse off than those who would have lived.

So far so good. Parfit demonstrates, however, that this answer applies only to 'same number cases' and not to 'different number cases'. In the former, whatever we decide to do, we can assume that the same number of people will later be born. In the latter category, into which most political decisions – certainly those of environmental policies – fall, whatever we decide to do affects not only the identity but also the number of the people who will later be born. Thus, the above utilitarian formula will not work in the cases of different numbers, whether as a principle of average utilitarianism or as a principle of total utilitarianism.

Suppose, first, that the utilitarian theorist suggests that it would be worse if those who lived were on an average worse off than those who would have lived. Suppose, also, that policy x ends up with a population of m people and an average happiness $h\,1$, whereas a policy y ends up with a population of n people ($n > m$), and an average happiness $h\,2$ ($h\,2 < h\,1$). In that case, using the formula, we would recommend policy x, whereas our intuition is not always to prefer a higher degree of average happiness and smaller populations to larger populations and lower average happiness. A good example is provided by Parfit: suppose that Adam and Eve were very happy, and that later generations were also happy, but less so. According to the average utility principle it would be better if only the very happy Adam and Eve had lived (Parfit 1984: 420–3). This is parallel to our argument in the section on population policies, where we discussed the unsatisfactory implications of average utilitarianism: i.e. if my child is going to be happy, but a little bit less happy than the average happy person in my society, then I should refrain from creating her.

A second interpretation of the formula is that of total utilitarianism: it would be worse if those who lived were worse off than those who would have lived. Parfit's answer is his well-known 'repugnant conclusion'. Suppose that policy x would lead to a population of n people, each having 10 units of happiness. A policy y would end up with a population of $2n$ people, each having 8 units of happiness. Total utilitarians, using the above principle, would ask us to follow policy y ($16n$ units of happiness being better than $10n$ units). While this conclusion sometimes corresponds to our intuition that it is better to have a somewhat larger society in which everyone is slightly less happy than a minute society in which the people are a bit happier, what would we say of a policy z which resulted in a population of 100n people, each person having half a unit of happiness? Oddly enough, total utilitarians, following the above principle, would opt for policy z rather than policy y or policy x. This is somewhat objectionable, and hence Parfit calls it the 'repugnant conclusion' (Parfit 1984: 387–8).

To sum up at this point, the argument is quite simple: as utilitarian person-regarding principles encounter unavoidable and insurmountable challenges, one must return to non-person-regarding principles. It is here that Stearns offers a proposal to rescue the total utilitarian theory by departing from person-regarding morality and relating the obligations that we have to 'future happiness' rather than to future persons (Stearns 1972). In doing so he shifts the commitment to one which maximizes future happiness, no matter to what persons this future happiness is assigned.

But one cannot produce happiness without relating it to persons. In one's interactions or communications with people, one increases or decreases the happiness of those people. If I take a balloon and blow it up, no happiness is produced or increased. But once I give the balloon to my child, his happiness is increased. If a particular melody causes me to be happy, it does not mean (although we say so) that the melody itself is a happy one. It is we who become happier, not the notes or tunes, nor the piano that they are played on. Happiness is something that persons experience or feel – or, unfortunately, sometimes do not – but it cannot stand alone, because happiness is inseparable from people and their feelings.

In general, we may conclude that the difficulties we experience in applying the utilitarian approach to our present context derive from the fact that the very existence of future people who are to serve as a basis of calculation depends on our current policies. How are we to decide on a policy that affects future people by calculating utilities when, at the same time, that very decision may affect their number, identity, or even their actual existence? The same applies to average utility: while we must seek to maximize the average utility of future persons, average utility may depend – among other things – on the number of people in the future. So, on the whole the utilitarian theory faces here an unresolvable difficulty with regard to population policies. Parfit's depletion cases indicate that these difficulties are also related to some other difficulties with regard to principles of distribution. And indeed, further difficulties come to life when one tackles questions of intergenerational distributive justice.

THE UTILITARIAN THEORY AND QUESTIONS
OF INTERGENERATIONAL DISTRIBUTION

The utilitarian says (a) that our actions should be directed to the maximum utility of all affected persons; and (b) that it is possible to calculate or measure personal utilities. When applying these arguments to questions of intergenerational justice, argument (a) becomes problematic because of the question of who the affected people are, and argument (b) is false because we have no tools for measuring or calculating personal utilities in this context. These difficulties not only lead us to absurdities with regard to obligations to future generations, but tell us nothing about what really matters – how much we should save or conserve, what we should do or how we should act for the sake of future people.

Let us start with the question of who the affected persons are. Although no utilitarian theorist has elaborated a precise principle of intergenerational justice, it is apparent that all contend that 'if X is a person, then X should be as happy as possible' (cf. Narveson 1967: 67), and this commits us to considering a person independent of her 'historic' time: i.e. we must distribute resources not only between present people but between all people, including future people as well.

Here the question arises, who are all these people? Those who are living and will continue to live? Or perhaps those who might live if we changed our policies? As we saw earlier, Narveson believes that only future persons, and not possible ones, should count. To the person who thinks that this implication of the person-regarding approach is too calculating, Narveson answers by asking whether it is not reasonable to insist on being told to whom we would be unkind or heartless (Narveson 1978: 52). Nevertheless, this is not a foolproof argument. Narveson's suggestion that, because of the person-regarding view of utilitarianism, we do not bear obligations to 'possible persons' stands in contradiction to the obligation which – according to the utilitarians – we have to a miserable child, which is not to conceive him. For if we do not conceive the miserable child, there would be no one to whom anything would be owed (cf. MacMahan 1981). So Bennet (1978) revises this argument: according to him, the question of whether a certain action is morally obligatory depends only upon the utilities of people who would exist if the action were not performed. Thus, conceiving a happy child is not obligatory because it depends only upon the utilities of people who would exist if the happy child were not conceived, i.e. upon the utilities of no one. On the other hand, by the same rationale 'not conceiving a miserable child' is morally obligatory. But while this is a brilliant argument in the intergenerational context, it is rather odd when applied to contemporaries (i.e. to the context of obligations within a single generation). Suppose, for example, that I have to decide whether giving a beggar my pound or offering shelter to the homeless person whom I come across, are morally obligatory. Suppose, further, that if I do not give the pound or offer shelter at my home, this person is likely to starve to death. But then he would not exist if the action were not performed, and therefore – according to Bennet – his utilities do not count. This seems to me wrong.

One can attempt to 'play' with the formula again and again, but eventually one has to admit that there is no utilitarian answer to the question of the affected persons in the intergenerational context, and that utilitarian principles cannot be applied to infinite and undetermined sizes of population. Even if utilitarians find an answer to the question of affected persons, they immediately face another difficulty regarding the nature of the objects of maximization in the intergenerational context. Here we encounter two major problems that are related to the distinction between objective and subjective utilitarianism.

While we often know, or at least have good reason to believe, that a certain act or policy will affect future generations, we rarely know the exact nature of these consequences. Since it is impossible to foresee their environment, it is impossible to predict the precise way future generations will be affected by or react to our policies and actions. Moreover, there are so many side events (events that have nothing to do with the agents or the object of an act) affecting the consequences of our policies that it is extremely unlikely that we are able to calculate or predict those consequences with any certainty, especially with regard to the remote future. Such calculations would be no more than rough guesses at best. Even devoted utilitarians admit that 'the future . . . is dim, largely because the potentialities of technological advance are unknown to us. This consideration . . . increases the difficulty of applying such an ethics' (Smart, in Smart and Williams 1973: 64). But the way Smart attempts to solve the problem ('Normally the utilitarian is able to assume that the remote effects of his actions tend rapidly to zero') is extremely cursory and oversimplifies the question. Such assertions are, environmentally speaking, irresponsible.

But there is more to this line of reasoning. Utilitarianism claims that we should maximize utility, in terms of satisfaction of preferences or desires. In fact, utility or happiness can be perceived in two ways: one can either claim that there is some kind of 'reality' and thus relate utility to some object that we, according to our values, think worth maximizing, or one can relate utility to the fulfilment of people's desires, as revealed by empirical tests or by common knowledge. In the former case one regards the criterion for utility as 'objective', inasmuch as it does not necessarily depend on personal tastes – as expressed by individuals or as shown in their behaviour – while in the latter instance maximum consideration is given to people's expressed tastes. So when one says that for Nancy state of affairs A has greater utility than state of affairs B, this can mean either that it *should* have greater utility for her (according to objective utilitarianism) or else that Nancy says, or her behaviour indicates, that it has greater utility for her (according to subjective utilitarianism). Thus, the philosopher R.M. Hare distinguishes between the actual preferences of the agents and 'perfectly prudent preferences' – what the agents would prefer if they were fully rational, informed and unconfused (Sen and Williams 1982: 23–38). But economists prefer not to use the term 'utility' at all, but rather 'preferences', especially 'revealed preferences', to describe preferences that can be measured (Sen 1961).

When we turn our attention to the intergenerational context, we may find ourselves in a strange situation. Suppose, first, that we follow objective utilitarianism. While utilitarians do not wish to dictate the needs, desires, norms, etc. of future generations, they may very well be doing so. If we contemporaries decide what 'utility' stands for, what the objects of maximization are, then we will, in effect, be imposing our tastes and values on future persons.

How does the utilitarian theorist deal with this conflict? If she follows objective utilitarianism she argues, broadly, that there are some preferences that are universal, or are acknowledged by every rational person. She therefore acts as if she were able to foresee and determine what should and will cause happiness or utility to future people, without regard for her own preferences. But she is consequently obliged to speak in very general terms, narrowing the range of possible causes of happiness or utility, or she will end up imposing her own values and preferences on future society. If, on the other hand, she draws a more detailed picture rather than broadly outlining their common, ordinary preferences, then all her calculations with regard to future people will nevertheless be according to *her* own beliefs. She is therefore revealed as much less tolerant and universal than she pretends to be. Moreover, she is in danger of conserving exactly the objects which future generations will most dislike.

My basic criticism – that the objective utilitarian dictates values to future people – could be taken as a general objection to objective utilitarianism as such. Any 'objective' utility principle reflects the personal values of the person who ascribes 'objectivity' to these utilities. But my argument refers to the specific context of inter-generational justice. Every notion of objective utility relies on conceptions of general human needs: for instance, good food, clean air, and health are regarded as human needs, and as such are said to create utility or happiness and are worth maximization. But there are more specific objects or activities (e.g. tracking in the Himalayas) that provide people with utility. Nevertheless, these activities are regarded as having this nature in relation to a certain cultural and historical context. People reflect on history and social experience and conclude that these are human needs in their time. Their intuition, then, is that these are objects or activities that are worth maximization and are likely to produce a good deal of utility. At the same time, however, since this intuition is only based on reflection on the social experience of the past and present and on current values, their intellectual integrity must convince these people that this intuition is not universal in the temporal sense. In other words, these people cannot claim that they know what human needs will be in the future: we cannot predict the nature of utility in the future, nor can we observe it.

Utilitarians have so far neglected this point, perhaps because the utilitarian evaluates moral and political questions as an outsider who stands outside the arena observing the players. She then tries to sympathize with all the players affected by an action, and calculates how to maximize utility. But, in this venture, our utilitarian is in danger of failing to recognize the variety of people who in the cause of time will be affected by an act. In this case, she fails to recognize that future persons are not necessarily similar to contemporary persons; they may have different preferences, values, sources of happiness, and objects that bring them utility. This means that a principle based on objective utility may well dictate values and preferences to future generations.

Let me clarify this point further. The objective utilitarian will say that she defines the objects of maximization as what future people *should* want to maximize. But since the values of the 'objective' utilitarian are not universal with regard to time, her claim cannot be considered a principle of 'objective' utility in the intergenerational context. In this case, it would mean that future people would get what it would be rational for them to want for themselves were they living *now*, rather than what they should desire in new, future circumstances. Eventually, then, future people may not be happy with the policies that we choose for them according to what we mistakenly and without proper information think would be rational for them to desire.

So much for objective utilitarianism. Now, if our utilitarian follows subjective utilitarianism, she must acknowledge the fact that she has no tools whatsoever to predict the tastes of the not-yet-born, and therefore has no means of deciding about utilities. While in the intragenerational context there is no difficulty in observing and measuring revealed preferences, it is obvious that the personal preferences and values of future persons are very likely to differ from our own. We are therefore incapable of envisaging future persons' preferences, desires, and forms of happiness.

At this point one can refer to an interesting theory which is sometimes used in support of both the objective and the subjective utilitarians. This theory, put forward by certain economists, maintains that it is plausible to predict tastes, which, however, have to be distinguished from preferences. Tastes, they claim, are more basic, and hence stable and universal, whereas preferences are expressions of temporary desires, dependent on prices, and as such are subject to change. In 1977 Stigler and Becker suggested treating tastes as basically unchanging and similar among different people:

> The venerable admonition not to quarrel over tastes is commonly interpreted as advice to terminate a dispute when it has been resolved into a difference of tastes, presumably because there is no further room for rational persuasion. Tastes are the unchallengeable axioms of a man's behaviour.... Tastes never change capriciously nor differ importantly between people.... (Tastes) are there, will be there next year and are the same to all men.
>
> (Stigler and Becker 1977: 76)

The argument develops: since all changes in preferences may be explained in economic terms through changes in prices and incomes, it is possible to develop tools for predicting preferences without reference to tastes at all. Moreover, the strength of the theory, according to these two scholars, is not its accurate reflection of reality, but rather that the hypothesis of stable tastes has yielded the most useful predictions about observable behaviour, and that 'no significant behaviour has been illuminated by assumptions of differences in tastes.' In other words, it does not matter whether or not the premises are true, or are a reflection of 'real life', but rather that using them makes the efforts of scientists to explain social phenomena more productive. But this methodology, while quite common among economists, is inapplicable to political thought. As Jon Elster argues, it seems anachronistic to attribute to premodern societies the preference patterns characteristic of ourselves. Moreover,

> There is a paradox here, that the staunchest defenders of the rational-actor approach should propose a theory having the undeniable effect of downgrading the importance of choice as compared to opportunities.
>
> (Elster 1984: 115 and note)

Admittedly, this is a methodological dispute, and I am not sure whether one can or should find a final answer to it. Nevertheless, I claim that Stigler and Becker's assumption cannot be taken seriously if it denies the possibility of changes in tastes over long periods of time, such as overgenerational changes. Woody Allen's film 'Sleeper' offers an apt and pertinent example: it portrays a person who is put to sleep and wakes up in the next century to find that behaviour, habits, political tendencies, and tastes have changed. But we do not have to turn to science fiction in order to realize that people's tastes, even the most basic ones, tend to change a great deal over long periods of time. This is true in art, literature, food, clothes, and so forth. Consider, moreover, the tremendous changes in religious attitudes. It goes without saying that religious beliefs are a matter of basic tastes rather than preferences and do not depend on prices. Only fifty years ago the percentage of religious Jews was much higher than it is now. This affected, among other things, the average number of children that Jews had. The same applies, as Barry mentions, to the Roman Catholic community in Quebec. There, for more than two centuries, the birth rate was 'close to the physical maximum', whereas now it is one of the lowest in North America (Barry 1982: 223–4). Changes in preferences (the number of children) are in this case a consequence of changes in tastes (religious beliefs).

Moreover, I am not quite sure that the utilitarian would want to follow his own distinction. Since preferences change dramatically over generations, and since they are unforeseeable, being a function of factors such as prices, income, etc., which are not known now, suppose we refer instead to tastes. But tastes, we are told, do not change over time. The implication in the overgenerational context is very conservative. The policy which is approved by utilitarianism today is also good for tomorrow. 'So what?' you may ask, 'not every theory has to be revolutionary.' But think of the environment: would you agree that the economic and environmental policies of the 1890s are good for the 1990s?

But, having contested the idea that tastes are static one should note that many utilitarians do, in fact, tend to acknowledge that tastes change. For instance, some utilitarians ask whether, in order to increase our want-satisfactions, all we have to do is to change our desires so that they conform to already-existing circumstances. This implies that these utilitarians can conceive of a situation where tastes change quite drastically. It could be argued that some aspects of the happiness of future people, such as health, are indeed foreseeable, but at the same time many other quite important aspects are not predictable and are likely to differ from ours, or at least be ranked differently. Indeed, a utilitarian might make the controversial claim that it is not worth saving particular goods or resources for future people, simply because a fortune will be invested in conserving resources which future people may very well not care about at all – and would that not be a waste?

One generation may think that salt herring is the most delicious food imaginable and, being a generous generation, may leave enough for future generations; but another generation may have a completely different taste, and think that herring stinks. Or consider the popular *Three Men in a Boat*, and Jerome K. Jerome's description of the china dog that ornaments the bedroom of his furnished lodgings:

> It is a white dog. Its eyes are blue. Its nose is a delicate red, with black spots. Its head is painfully erect, and its expression is amiability carried to the verge of imbecility. I do not admire it myself. Considered as a work of art, I may say it irritates me. Thoughtless friends jeer at it, and even my landlady herself has no admiration for it, and excuses its presence by the circumstances that her aunt gave it to her. But in two hundred years' time it is more than probable that that dog will be dug up from somewhere or other, minus its legs, and with its tail broken,

and will be sold for old china, and put in a glass cabinet. And people will pass it round and admire it. They will be struck by the wonderful depth of the colour on the nose.[5]

It may appear that I am inconsistent in arguing for the importance of the idea of the good and of the community in the first two chapters, and then teasing the utilitarians for not being able to maintain their universalism. But I still think that the idea of the good and the community play an important role in the social and political sphere. However, the point is that theories and theorists have to be consistent, and that utilitarianism fails to be consistent in the intergenerational context because it is forced to contradict its most important premises. The utilitarian cannot preach universalism and temporal impartiality in the intragenerational context and then neglect the utilities of some parts of the population in the intergenerational context.

However, we are still left with another question: to what, then, are we obligated? How much should we pass on to future generations and how much can we consume or pollute without neglecting our obligations? That utilitarianism is silent about distribution is not a new assertion (Rawls 1973: 278), so I shall refrain from further detail, except to state that this applies to the intergenerational case as well. The principle of maximizing utility over generations says nothing about what the distribution of resources should be, beyond the fact that the distribution is dictated by the overall goal. We have not got the slightest clue how much we should save for future people, bearing in mind that saving for the sake of future people might contradict the principle of maximizing utilities of contemporaries. The implications of this failure in the intergenerational context are obnoxious: We have already seen, while discussing Parfit's 'depletion' paradox, that a consistent interpretation of the utilitarian intergenerational principle might lead one to the conclusion that we have no obligation whatsoever to future generations. And yet again, a different reading might offer the suggestion that utilitarianism demands too much from us, too heavy a sacrifice.

Actually, Sidgwick was the first utilitarian philosopher to acknowledge difficulties on this point, although he did not analyse it profoundly (Sidgwick 1981 (1874): 414). 'How far', he asked 'are we to consider the interests of posterity when they seem to conflict with those of existing human beings?' And yet, he immediately insisted 'the time at which a man exists cannot affect the value of his happiness from a universal point of view'. So one wishes to sustain environmental policies – i.e. to find the equilibrium between our obligations to posterity and the improved welfare of our contemporaries – while at the same time the utilitarian is committed to temporal universalism. This demands too much from us contemporaries, since almost every act that we perform now could damage the interests of or cause pain to those who will live in the future. And since there will be many more future persons than present ones, we shall always be in a position of giving priority to their utilities. Assuming that an investment is productive and is used wisely by subsequent generations, the bigger the initial investment is, the larger is the total aggregate utility or profit. In order to maximize the aggregate utility over generations, the first generations should thus reduce their standard of living to a minimum, investing all the rest.

This is not only unfair, it is also paradoxical. After the first generation has done its job and played its due part in the process, the second generation finds itself in the same situation as the first one; i.e. the second generation is obliged to save and invest the most it can, thereby reducing its own standard of living. This continues with every generation until we reach the point when a generation can foresee that the end of mankind is only so far ahead. Each generation should save and conserve as much as it can, consuming the least that it can (i.e. almost nothing). While there are some very radical Greens or 'deep ecologists' who sometimes support this demand because, for instance, it implies getting rid of all industry,[6] it is generally regarded as unreasonable. Remember that we want people to become greener and we are not likely to attract them by asking them to make a sacrifice which is contrary to the psychological basis of utilitarianism, which is hedonism.[7]

A utilitarian could still defend her theory by claiming that, since there is a slight, but more than zero chance, that life on earth could be terminated by a catastrophe, an element of doubt whether each new generation will exist at all should be built into the argument. We should therefore discount the effects of our policies on future generations and give more weight to our obligations to fellow contemporaries. But this might cause us to ignore very dangerous actions simply because their effect are most likely to be manifested in the remote future.[8] Or suppose that by doing x we could either prevent a minor catastrophe in the present or prevent a major disaster in the remote future. Those taking account of probability factors will prevent the minor catastrophe in the present, allowing the chance of a terrible disaster later (cf. Parfit 1984: 485).

Part of our obligation to future generations is to prevent such fatal catastrophes as far as we can especially when nuclear and toxic waste are concerned. After all, one cannot claim that all people count equally no matter when they live and at the same time argue that there are policies which may cause death to future people but are justified because they increase the welfare of contemporaries. The lives of future people are 'non-tradable' to use Goodin's expression (1982). He is prepared to accept the discount technique only if it is excluded from the spheres of 'non-tradable goods', goods that cannot be evaluated in terms of money or any material good. In this sense, every development policy that sacrifices the lives of some future people can only be justified in terms of saving the lives of other future people or contemporaries. But any discount rate is outrageous when a policy is likely to cost some future lives and will not at the same time save some lives. Finally, this discount rationale is hazardous because, once we start discounting, we might end up discounting in self-serving ways, giving priority to the interests of contemporaries over the interests of future people and justifying this with the discount technique. In other words, we cannot be relied on always to discount fairly.

So when the utilitarian theory is applied to the intergenerational context both its total and average interpretations face difficulties which involve the question of the obligation to conceive, or to refrain from conceiving, children in an attempt to find a just population policy, even before considering any principle of intergenerational distributive justice. Some even employ a utilitarian calculation to prove that it is better if we do not have children, although many of us believe that the existence of people in the future is to be sought even if it does not maximize happiness (cf. Barry 1977a: 283–4).

Following the difficulties with population policies, utilitarians are faced with further difficulties when tackling issues of intergenerational distribution, the most important of which is that they either neglect future generations or demand too much from present ones. They can give no clear advice as to what distribution over generations should be like. Perhaps J.P. Surber is correct in saying that the issue of environmental policies is a dimension of our problem that is wholly outside the range of the utilitarian point of view (Surber 1977).

4

CONTRACTARIAN THEORIES OF INTERGENERATIONAL JUSTICE

When God created the first man he showed him all the trees in Eden and said: Look how beautiful they are. So take care not to ruin them, because if you do – no one will restore it after you.

Midrash

INTRODUCTION

The original aim of classical contractarian theorists was to legitimize political obligations and to show that their acceptance could be justified by rational individuals. In recent decades we have witnessed an interesting attempt to widen and broaden the contractarian theory so that it might serve as a basis for a theory of distributive justice. Those who enter the contract are assumed to be rational, self-interested persons who regard their identities as existing independently of society and who hold some natural rights. All the same, the contractarian argues, it is rational for them to restrict their rights in some spheres in order to gain security or economic advantages or in order to promote justice. In these spheres they will be bound only to what they have explicitly or tacitly agreed upon. Thus, the contemporary contractarian theorist argues that economic and social co-operation and a system of social justice can be voluntarily accepted by all members of society. In fact, this is the beauty of contractarianism, that although its premises are individualistic it aims to justify social co-operation.

In the sphere of environmental ethics, the contractarian theorist cannot bring in non-human animals, plants, or monuments to sign a contract. Therefore Brennan argues that contractarianism fails to 'be ecological' (Brennan 1988: 170–1, 178–82). But it is tempting to try to approach the issue of the environment using the contractarian method. If one succeeded in this, human beings would then have an agreement with respect to the environment (Manning 1981; Singer B. 1988). Here, however, I intend to focus on the contractarian approach to intergenerational justice. Indeed, the idea of one generation having obligations to future generations, derived from the rationale of a hypothetical agreement, is not a new one. For example, the following story is found in the Jewish Talmud. A young man once saw an old man planting a carob tree by the side of the road. He asked the old man how many years it would take the tree to bear fruit. 'Seventy,' the old man replied and kept on with his work. 'Are you sure you will live long enough to eat the fruit?' the young man asked. The old man looked at him and replied: 'When I came into the world, I found it planted with carob trees. Just as my ancestors planted for me, so shall I plant for posterity' (Ta'anit, 23). Behind the old man's words lay a belief in implicit obligations to future generations derived from a tacit agreement. It is commonly argued that we have obligations to posterity because we have received certain goods from our predecessors in return for which we are virtually obliged and committed to maintain the chain. And yet, the oddity of the idea of an intergenerational contract can be summarized in Stearns' words: 'Why should there be obligations to future generations? We have made no commitment to them. We have entered no social compacts with them' (Stearns 1972). However, more sophisticated contractarian arguments for obligations to future generations do exist, of which I shall examine here two examples: the theories of Gauthier and Rawls. These two theories in fact represent two types of general contractarian theory (Barry 1989).[1] Broadly speaking, one tradition is related to Glaucon, Hobbes, Hume, the game theorists, and Gauthier, amongst others, and is described by Barry as that of the 'mutual advantage' theories. The other is related to the Stoics, the Enlightenment – especially Kant – and Rawls, and is described by Barry as that of the theories of 'impartiality'.

Both traditions share two main arguments: (a) questions of justice arise when there is a conflict of interests, and (b) justice is that on which everyone can in principle reach rational agreement (Barry 1989: 7). However, the two traditions differ in their responses to three questions: What is justice? Why be just? And, how are the demands of justice determined? To the question of what justice is, the first tradition responds that it is a necessity and a compromise. To the question of why one should be just, the answer lies in self-interest: co-operation produces better results, and thus people compromise in order to achieve co-operation. In fact, no special motive for behaving justly should be invoked, because 'justice is simply rational prudence pursued in contexts where the cooperation . . . of other people is a condition for our being able to get what we want' (Barry 1989: 6–7). To the question of how we determine the demands of justice, the response given by the first tradition is mutual advantage: people accept a certain distribution when they cannot reasonably expect to get any more. For this reason 'history' (the state of affairs which existed before any bargaining took place) is important in this theory, because the level at which one would not expect to get more is a consequence of what one has initially, i.e. one's original bargaining power. Therefore the agreement reflects differences in the strength of the original bargaining positions.

The second tradition – justice as impartiality – gives different answers to these questions. Justice is not a matter of necessity and compromise but rather an impartial attitude on the part of all relevant persons, or consideration of a question from an impartial perspective. In other words, justice consists of putting oneself in the other person's shoes. The motive for acting justly, then, is not self-interest but rather defending a principle without any appeal to personal advantage: one would have reason to accept it no matter who one is (cf. Scanlon 1982: 120). Thus, justice is unrelated to bargaining power and it requires the agreement to be one in which the relative strength of the parties concerned has no influence on the just solution. People accept a just state of affairs when they cannot reasonably claim more (Barry 1989: 8).

Now Gauthier, often termed 'neo-Hobbesian' by other scholars, is a representative of the theory of justice as mutual advantage. In Rawls, on the other hand, one finds some elements of each tradition. In the case of both schools, I argue that we cannot conceive of a principle of *intergenerational* justice or determine obligations to future people compatibly with contractarian premises.

BARGAINING WITH THE NOT-YET-BORN? THEORIES OF MUTUAL ADVANTAGE AND THE MULTIGENERATIONAL CONTEXT

According to the 'mutual advantage' theory, the rationale of relations within social institutions is contractarian (Gauthier 1977: 135). Thus bargaining principles determine the allocation of goods to persons on the basis of their hypothetical previous agreement, as though it were arrived at before any goods were produced. Rational agents, it is argued, would reach agreement in a bargain over the distribution of goods if they first reached agreement on how much each one would concede so that others would be willing to co-operate. Everyone would want for themselves all that could be gained through co-operation, and would thus want the others to make concessions. A reasonable agreement is thus one in which each agent is left with the same proportional concession from a maximum gain.

Gauthier argues that the solution to the bargaining is the 'minimax relative concession'.

> Given a range of outcomes, each of which requires concessions by some or all persons if it is to be selected, then an outcome [will] be selected only if the greatest or maximum relative concession it requires is as small as possible, or a minimum, that is, is no greater than the maximum relative concession required by every other outcome.
>
> (Gauthier 1986: 137)

Gauthier's principle, then, requires the smallest possible equal concessions, in relative terms, from the bargainers. Now some game theorists argue that bargaining situations have more than one solution because we cannot predict what rational agents will agree upon. On the other hand, Nash (1950) contends that there is one solution to bargaining, which differs from Gauthier's solution. However, for our purpose it does not matter what the bargaining solution is. The point is that the mutual advantage contractarian believes that there is a certain principle which the rational agent will agree upon.

Turning now to the question of intergenerational bargaining, it seems that this concept of justice excludes cases of intergenerational relations because the principles of justice are those of social choice (Gauthier 1978a) and where there is no element of social choice (as in the case of the not-yet-born) there is no room for justice. Yet Gauthier claims that there is a 'fair bargaining among generations'. Since each of us interacts simultaneously with older and younger persons we create a 'continuous thread of interaction extending from the most remote human past to the farthest future of our kind' (Gauthier 1986: 289). The difficulty of entering into contracts with not-yet-existing people is sidestepped because the contract is made between several generations who live at the same time. Generations A, B, and C have, so to speak, a sort of contract, which is extended to generations B, C, and D, and then to C, D, and E, and so on. When an older generation decides to co-operate with a younger one – because they are contemporaries and because it recognizes that through co-operation production will increase – the younger one will only agree to a contract likely to be accepted by the even younger (future) generations. The result is a chain connection between generations:

> No matter when one lives, one should expect the same relative benefits from interaction with one's fellows as were enjoyed by one's predecessors and as will be enjoyed in turn by one's successors. The need to continue any agreement as time passes, to extend it to those who are born as it ceases for those who die, ensures that among rational persons, the term must remain constant.
>
> (Gauthier 1986: 299)

At first sight, this chain of generations solves another difficulty: the bargaining theory usually refers to a finite set of actors; but, in the intergenerational context, there is an infinite number of actors: we must take into account all future generations. Gauthier overcomes this difficulty by introducing the idea of a chain of generations in which every three generations that exist at one and the same time form an agreement which is then passed on.

As for the substance of intergenerational co-operation, it must relate to the environment and, in this context, we can speak of two elements: one involves the factors governing inheritance (including aesthetic landscapes, etc.), and the other involves kinds of investments (including sustainable development, or the setting aside of natural resources). With regard to inheritance, the contractarian claims that if an individual acquires the right to the exclusive use of a certain good, then she is entitled to dispose of that right as she pleases, and even to bequeath it to any other person. So there are 'temporally open-ended rights' which are gained through a bequest rather than through market exchange.

Now, what should the rate of investment be? If investment is for the sake of sustainable development, it takes the form of investing a portion of the present production as capital for future production rather than using it for present consumption, and by limiting depletion of resources so that future generations can use them as well. But this, of course, diminishes the present supply, and since saving makes more goods available in the future than could be provided at present, why should those with fewer goods (previous generations) transfer them to those with more (future generations)? Gauthier's answer is that in a bargain between generations 'there is no single transferable good to be shared among all, but instead there is a steadily increasing good to be shared in proportionally equal amounts' (Gauthier 1986: 304). Thus, by viewing society as a bargain in which 'the terms remain constant over time, so that each generation offers its successor the same agreement that it accepted from its predecessor' in terms of relative concessions, we can arrive at a clear idea of justice between generations (Gauthier 1986: 304).

But a few general factors essential to the contractarian model of justice as mutual benefit are absent from intergenerational relations, and their absence frustrates the attempt to approach intergenerational justice as a matter of a 'mutual-advantage contract'. These include equality of power; the fact that the reason for entering the contract is the reason for remaining in it; the function of constraint exercised by society; reciprocity. Let us examine these characteristics in the intergenerational context.

It has long been argued by mutual-advantage contractarians that justice is a virtue only if certain 'circumstances of justice' obtain: (a) a rough equality in the powers and capacities of the parties concerned; (b) a moderate scarcity (goods are available, yet moderately scarce, and hence social co-operation is not pointless); (c) there is a conflict of interests due to the fact that people are not indifferent to the distribution of benefits resulting from co-operation – conflict exists together with an identity of interests, since all benefit from social co-operation.[2] I shall not discuss the second and third conditions. Whether or not they will be relevant in the future is either impossible to ascertain or a matter of empirical knowledge which I believe is not yet available. For instance, will there be moderate scarcity? For some commodities at least, in particular non-renewable resources such as oil, we are quite certain that the scarcity will become less and less moderate. However, we are able to discuss equality of power between generations.

Equality of power means that individuals are 'roughly similar in physical and mental powers; or, at any rate, their capacities are comparable in that no one among them can dominate the rest' (Rawls 1973: 127). The parties to the agreement 'would enforce their will on each other if they could, but ... in view of the equality of forces amongst them and for the sake of their own peace and security, acknowledge certain forms of conduct insofar as prudence seems to require' (Rawls 1958: 174). This description of equality of power between members of society does not apply to the relations between distant generations, however. Through the actions of many individuals we contemporaries decide on policies of distribution, we decide what to conserve, or determine how many future people there will be. But how can future generations affect our welfare? How can future people determine how many of us will live? Indeed, Goodin makes an interesting attempt to derive obligations to future generations from the very difference in power between the generations. The vulnerability of future generations, the fact that they are completely dependent upon us to provide help or to prevent harm, provides the reason for our obligations to them (Goodin 1985: 277).

Yet the argument of equality of power between generations should not be rejected off-hand. The contractarian might, for instance, claim that, although contemporaries are superior to future generations in some ways, the latter have superiority of power in others; or the contractarian might argue that future generations will have power over even later future generations, and hence a 'different' sort of equality of power will exist. Let us examine these arguments.

Those arguing in favour of an equality of power would claim that future generations are in a position to affect us because they can judge and criticize our behaviour, intentions, and actions, and evaluate projects we have created and developed: they have the power to decide how others will perceive what we have done. As I have already suggested in previous chapters all this is quite correct, but where mutual advantage is concerned it can only qualify the difference in power. It is not at all *equivalent* to the difference in power that we contemporaries have in relation to future generations. Future people will not have the power to stop us polluting water resources or depleting rain forests. Moreover, by the use of genetic engineering we can today affect the identities and numbers of future persons, decide who and how many they will be and, more or less, what they will be like. We even have the power to decide whether there actually will be any future persons, whereas future people will never have the power to stop us deciding not to continue human existence on earth by not reproducing. In this sense, the asymmetry of power between the generations is unquestionable.

Contractarian theorists may then employ another strategy. They may argue that the difference in power between two generations – say, C and D – is neutralized and compensated by the difference in power between generations D and E, which is again neutralized by the difference between E and F, and so on. Hence 'duties do meet rights [though] not in respect of the same persons' (Laslet 1979: 48). But if generation A is superior to B, and B is compensated by being superior to C, then, according to this argument, A must be superior to C, which is compensated by being superior to E. And since A is superior to C and C is superior to E, then A is superior to E.

Now suppose that we have a history of eight generations, A, B, C, D, E, F, G and H. Let us examine the situation of generation F (s ≡ 'superior in power to'):

> AsF
> BsF
> CsF
> DsF   FsH
> EsF   FsG

Only the superiority of D and E to F are compensated for, and, of course, generation G is even farther removed from equality of power with the other generations. Thus, suppose n is the number of generations in history. If n is an even number, then the last $n/2$ generations will suffer a lack of equality of power; and if n is an odd number, then the last $(n - 1)/2$ generations will suffer a lack of equality of power. A chain of relationships of this kind cannot replace equality in power in the intergenerational context. In other words, if contractarian theorists claim that justice is a virtue only when the circumstances for justice exist, they will face a problem because there can be no equality of power between generations that live at different times.

Another essential feature of the contract theory is the idea that the reasons for entering into the contract must be the same as the reasons for 'maintaining the society created thereby' (Gauthier 1977: 139). This is intuitive within one generation, but not between generations. In order to be attractive, any contract must follow two rules.

(a) Its outcome – either with regard to quality of environment or in any other way (e.g. with regard to security) – should be optimal in the sense used by Pareto. That is, any alternative outcome which would better the state of one agent would be worse for another agent.
(b) All the participants should view the outcome of the contract as better than the 'natural outcome', i.e. the outcome of actions taken before (or in the absence of) an agreement.

In the intergenerational context, the state of nature is a situation in which no generations save, and all exploit resources as much as they please, pollute the air, produce radioactive waste, damage the ozone layer, and so forth. A contract implies obligations and hence all generations which enter into a contract agree to be sparing with resources, to conserve, save money, and so on. They all wish to enter into the contract because all generations benefit by being protected against extravagant predecessors – but once the contract has been implemented, why should one stay in it? Is it irrational to withdraw from an intergenerational contract *ex post*? We entered into the contract because, if every generation depleted all it produced, all generations, including ours, would be worse off; yet, this is not, and cannot be, the reason for remaining in the contract, because we have already enjoyed our predecessors' savings and acts of conservation, and we cannot enjoy them again.

Thus, we must obligate all generations to remain in the contract if we want to maintain it. But what can force them to do so? Within a single generation this is effected either by a sense of reciprocity or by a reiteration of the bargain, or by certain constraints, whether internal (i.e. conscience) or external (the state and its institutions). These do not exist in the intergenerational context. Reciprocity is in doubt (see below), there is no reiteration for the same agent (or generation), and no constraints compatible with the contractarian premises of self-interest or even mutual hostility[3] exist in the intergenerational context. As for external constraints (e.g. authority), in the intragenerational context the state and its apparatus play the role of the constraining element. Police, the judicial system, laws form the 'coercive powers' that, in Hobbes's words 'bridle men's passions'. But in the intergenerational context such institutions represent and advance the interests of the current generation only. Indeed, some members of the Green movement argue that this is *the* problem of environmental conservation, and suggestions as to the means for intergenerational constraints have been put forward, e.g. an ombudsmen for future generations, trust funds for posterity, and so forth (Weiss 1986). But there are no 'sanctions' between generations, and there is no way we can practice such sanctions, simply because the future person or future society cannot materialize in the past and apply such sanctions.

Much more important, one finds that reciprocity is absent in this context. Those who enter into a contract should have a sense of a reciprocal advantage to those who are subject to the contract, because then they are very likely to reach agreement upon principles of justice. By the same token, if the sense of reciprocity is absent, it is unlikely that people will enter into a contract at all or, if they do enter it, that they will uphold it. Reciprocity, then, is the motive for maintaining a contract. One must ask: is the concept of reciprocity applicable to the case of *intergenerational* justice? Annette Baier thinks that it is (A. Baier 1981). She relates obligations to posterity to the obligation to pass on what we have received from previous generations. Indeed, this was the case of the old man who planted a carob tree. Yet it is, after all, quite clear that after benefiting from a contract with past generations, it is rational and advantageous to abandon it. So is there reciprocity in the intergenerational context?

There are two interpretations of reciprocity to be discussed. According to one, reciprocity exists when there is mutual advantage; according to the other, reciprocity exists when there is some kind of fair play. Looking at the first concept, contractarians may defend the idea of mutual benefit between generations by arguing along these lines: the interests of future generation E are represented by C, the youngest generation to enter the agreement, because it knows that it would be faced with an agreement with E when it (C) becomes the oldest generation. Thus A has to consider E, or else A will never reach an agreement with C. The same applies to further future generations, but it involves a few more interactions between generations, a few more links in the chain. But although initially plausible, this argument is not ultimately convincing. Imagine the following conversation:

Generation C (to E): 'Let us co-operate and make an agreement Q.'

Generation E (to C): 'But you had a better agreement with A and B. You had agreement P and I want P too.'

Generation C (to E): 'Well, sorry. Take it or leave it. I have already benefited from P. I am offering you Q, because with it I shall be in a better position than now. But I am not desperate to have it, since I have already benefited from P, and the marginal utility of another agreement (Q) for me is not high.'

Now, it would be definitely irrational for E not to co-operate at all. So E accepts Q as a better alternative to no co-operation at all. Eventually, the contractarian may rightly argue, generations C, D, and E will reach an agreement. Nevertheless, not only is there no guarantee that it will be the same agreement as generations A, B, and C had (contract P), but we also expect generation C to propose a different agreement, and generations D and E to accept it, if they behave rationally. There will be no genuine mutual advantage if contract P is continued: generation C will not regard it as a benefit for itself. In Gauthier's terms, contract P will not reflect equal relative concessions. If, on the other hand, another contract is signed by these three generations (which is what the scenario suggests), then the theory fails to supply us with an ongoing transgenerational contract, or to justify obligations between distant generations. Generations A, B, and C may have an agreement to ban the ivory trade, but, after enjoying it, generation C would tell generations D and E that the new contract would allow limited trade, and D and E would have to accept the new terms, because otherwise they are in danger of C quitting the negotiations and doing whatever it wants to do. The conclusion is that rational behaviour ('a person acts rationally if and only if she seeks her greatest interest or benefit', (Gauthier 1986: 7)), introduced by the contractarian as a constraint that ensures mutual benefit in the intragenerational context, will not do the job in the intergenerational case. In fact, it might do just the opposite.

Let us illustrate this claim by imagining one is driving on the M40 from London to Oxford.[4] Each car is closed (it is a typically English day) and no driver is involved in the affairs and interests of any other driver. On the twenty-fifth mile, a long line of traffic begins, because, strangely enough, Arsenal is playing Liverpool in a friendly game right next to the road. As he or she passes that spot, each driver wants to slow down and watch the teams playing for a few seconds. But this would make people late for their appointments, for work, or for getting home, so they would rather that no one watched the game and that the traffic went on. What is needed is an intertemporal contract between all the drivers. They should agree that as each driver passes the players he or she will ignore them and go on driving. The first driver does so, as does the second, and so on until the ninetieth. This driver is more sophisticated, so as she passes the football match she knows that she has already benefited from the contract. She is not going to be late if she slows down for a few seconds to watch the big stars. And why should she care about the drivers behind her? She knows nothing about them, and they can in no way affect her or punish her for her behaviour, unless they are all going to get into similar situations again and again. In our story it would be like driving along a circular track, which is the reiteration mentioned above. And yet, this is not the case in intergenerational relations, nor here in our story: an intertemporal contract is quite different from a simple one.

However, there is another concept of reciprocity which contractarian theorists may defend in the intergenerational context, according to which much of the good that we receive is produced by people whom we do not know or see – not only in past generations, but also at the present time, e.g. those who live far away, perhaps in other countries. And yet, the contractarian would argue, reciprocity does exist, rooted in the sense of fair play. The obligation to reciprocate arises 'whenever we have received a good for which some sort of fitting and proportional return is possible, and it is often perfectly fitting to make our returns to people other than those who have benefited us' (Becker 1986: 230–1; Rawls 1973: 290).

Now, compare this notion of reciprocity with the reciprocity between two people, Jack and Jill. Jill sells cars and Jack deals in seat belts. They buy and sell from each other and send customers to each other; one does not cheat the other; they practice 'play fair'. But this notion of reciprocity is direct (second party) and specific, whereas reciprocity with future generations, which involves past generations (we owe future generations what we received from past generations, because of what we received from past generations), becomes abstract and third-party reciprocity, involving two groups of non-existing persons: past generations and future persons. In addition, there are cases in which this kind of reciprocity (B getting from A and reciprocally giving to C) will not be relevant. First, even if previous generations were a gang of misers and left us literally nothing, or seriously damaged the environment, polluted the soil, and so on, many people believe that we still have obligations to future generations and should refrain from polluting and damaging the environment for their sake. In any event, the fact that we were not treated justly by previous generations is no pretext for treating future generations unjustly. (Thus B gets nothing from A but nevertheless gives to C.) Second, in some cases our predecessors left us something which they expected *us* to consume, e.g. gifts. Not every time we receive something are we expected to reciprocate by giving the same to others. It is inconceivable that, when I suddenly get a toffee apple, my enjoyment of the apple creates 'even the tiniest *prima facie* obligation to distribute toffee apples to others' (Barry 1979). (Thus B gets from A but must not necessarily give to C.) These cases suggest that obligations to posterity do not necessarily always originate in the deeds of previous generations.

My objection, then, to the notion of reciprocity as fair play is that it is too vague and therefore does not help us establish an equilibrium between our obligations to future people and our obligations to contemporaries. If reciprocity is defined in this way, then there is no difference between what we receive from contemporaries and what we have received from past generations. Must I pass on to future generations, also as a matter of reciprocity, what I have received from you, a contemporary person? Why shouldn't I reciprocate past generations by giving to you, who are present, rather than to future people? In the final analysis, you exist here and now; I'd better 'pay my bill' quickly rather than wait for future people. What is the justification for giving to future people rather than present ones?

THEORIES OF JUSTICE AS IMPARTIALITY AND INTERGENERATIONAL JUSTICE; RAWLS'S SAVING PRINCIPLE

Thus far we have explored the limitations of the notion of mutual advantage in the intergenerational context. But a different notion of justice within the contractarian school is that of justice as an impartial identification with the interests of everyone, of which Rawls's theory is the most widely discussed example. One of its main characteristics is the assumption that, in deciding upon principles of justice, we should not be influenced by our knowledge of what makes us different from others, nor by our concept of what constitutes the good life. Rawls therefore posits a 'veil of ignorance' to hide all irrelevant information. From this 'original position', Rawls believes, all rational people will choose according to the maximin strategy: i.e. since one cannot assess one's real situation, one will ensure that the situation of the least advantaged will be maximized. In other words, one will choose principles that will prevent one from finding oneself in a 'catastrophic' situation; one will adopt the alternative the worst outcome of which is superior to the worst outcomes of the other alternatives.[5] This strategy results in two principles of justice being chosen: equal liberty for all, and a difference principle according to which social and economic inequalities are justified only if they are to the greatest benefit of the least advantaged (Rawls 1973: 302).

Rawls asserts that our relations with animals, plants, or the environment in general lie outside the scope of the theory of justice, because it does not seem possible to extend the idea of a contract to include animals, trees, and so forth (Rawls 1973: 512). Instead, he suggests that our relations to animals and nature would seem to 'depend upon a theory of the natural order and our place in it' – a task, then, for metaphysics.[6] But Rawls does advance an argument in favour of transgenerational savings; since he is egalitarian, it is surprising that he thinks in terms of accumulation. Why should there not be equality between all generations? Why should future generations have more than contemporaries? The answer seems to lie in Rawls's observation that we contemporaries harm future generations by damaging the environment. Accordingly, the saving principle is intended to compensate future generations for this damage. In this way, Rawls offers us an anthropocentric theory for relations with the environment. Let us, then, explore this saving principle.

Rawls's premise is that setting the social minimum will concern not only one generation but its successors as well. He then argues that each generation must not only preserve the gains of culture and civilization but must also, in its own period, put aside a suitable amount of real capital accumulation (Rawls 1973: 225). This is what he calls the 'saving principle'.

> In any generation, their expectations are to be maximized subject to the condition of putting aside the savings that would be acknowledged . . . Of course, the savings of the less favoured need not be done by their taking an active part in the investment process. Rather it normally consists of their approving of the economic and other arrangements necessary for the appropriate accumulation. Saving is achieved by accepting as a political judgement those policies designed to improve the standard of life of later generations of the least advantaged.
>
> (Rawls 1973: 292–3)[7]

The additional principle is required in the case of intergenerational justice because the 'difference principle does not apply to the saving principle', since 'there is no way for later generations to improve the situation of the least fortunate first generation' (Rawls 1973: 291). Moreover, the difference principle would require no saving at all, since in circumstances of progress the first generation is the least advantaged.

But why do we decide upon a saving principle? Those in the original position are regarded by Rawls as having a kind of family relationship with their immediate successors (Rawls 1973: 292). Thus for every future person there is someone who cares about her or him in the present generation, i.e. among those in the original position. But since Rawls has never previously said he regarded these people as representatives of a family, he has to explain and justify this. He does so by adjusting the motivation principle, i.e. the reason for entering the original position in the first place. All those in the original position acknowledge the psychological assumption that, as fathers, they are concerned about the welfare of their offspring.[8] In this way, Rawls believes, a decision in favour of the saving principle will be taken. Or will it?

If the contractarian follows theories of impartiality, then justice should not reflect any original difference in power – which is what Rawls terms a fair state of affairs. The question that immediately arises is whether the contractarian can apply this fairness in the inter-generational context, and to answer this we must examine three elements of Rawls's theory: the primary goods (are they relevant in the intergenerational context?); the motivation assumption (is it fair?); the extension of the original position to include future people as well (is this feasible?). Let us start, then, with the concept of primary goods.

Contractarian theorists assert that it is fair to ask people to follow rules or principles only if they have agreed upon them. Since, in practice, the theorists cannot ask everyone what they would agree upon, they conceive principles that would be reasonably consented to by everybody. In the original position, every participant is given a 'veto'; if he or she does not agree with the principles, then they are not accepted. So the contractarian theorist must imagine what future people would reasonably accept, in the absence of sufficient or adequate information about such people.

At first glance it seems that Rawls can deal with this problem by a combination of the idea of the veil of ignorance and the notion of primary goods. In Rawls's original position, information about personal preferences or tastes is not needed; on the contrary, it is considered wrong to decide on principles of justice according to knowledge of this kind. Thus the participants' veto does not reflect their real interests, derived from their being specific persons with unique characters, particular ideas of the good life, and so forth. Rather, the veto is a reflection of what the participants think the interests of an 'abstract' person would be. The latter is perceived as someone who would like to get as much as possible from Rawls's list of primary goods. The person knows that her ability to achieve whatever she wants or desires is greater if she has more primary goods.

Superficially, therefore, the contractarian may avoid the problem of a lack of information about future people by means of this device: i.e. by claiming that the abstract person represents people from all generations and that these primary goods are universal in the temporal sense as well. Let us then examine the concept of primary goods more carefully. There are two ways to interpret the notion 'primary goods'. One is to assert that, empirically, these are whatever people consider to be primary goods, i.e. goods of which one should have as much as possible for whatever purpose one wants; the other is to claim, as Rawls has recently done, that this notion derives from an 'idea of the person'. If the contractarian follows the first interpretation, then the claim that every conception of the good could be advanced by means of primary goods is only partly true and is partly spurious, as has been repeatedly argued with respect to contemporary people.[9] This limits the use of the notion of primary goods in a political theory based on neutrality, especially if it refers to future people: who is able to predict what their primary goods will be? Perhaps a few goods are likely to reappear in every generation's 'list', but perceptions of primary goods change over time. At first there are people's desires; then theories about the distribution of goods are formulated; subsequently, a certain distribution takes place; people reflect on what they possess; new technologies and exchanges of ideas and tastes come as inputs to this reflection. The result is that people have different and new desires, and a change in primary goods may come about. So when changes in the environment, technology, and social structure are as rapid and extreme as they are nowadays, who is to guarantee that these primary goods will remain the same? If Rawls's concept of primary goods is empirically based, if Rawls looks around him and draws up this list, then these goods cannot be viewed as universal, not merely in a sociological sense but also in a temporal sense. This compounds the difficulty with the idea of primary goods, once it is used in the intergenerational context; in fact this raises a similar difficulty to the one discussed in Chapter 3 about the object of utility.[10]

However, there is another interpretation of the concept of primary goods. After *Theory of Justice* had been completed, Rawls redefined primary goods as deriving from an idea of 'the person', or the moral personality.[11] Indeed, says Rawls, 'citizens do not affirm the same rational conception of the good, complete in all its essentials and especially its final ends and loyalties' (Rawls 1982: 161). Nevertheless, a partial similarity of citizens' conceptions of the good is sufficient for the promotion of political and social justice. Thus, the idea of the primary goods – the basic liberties, freedom of movement, and choice of occupation against a background of diverse opportunities; powers and prerogatives of office and positions of responsibility, income and wealth, and the social bases of self-respect – comes to be accepted on the basis of a conception of a person with a motivation of the highest order: namely, to exercise the two functions of the moral personality – providing a sense of right and justice and the capacity to decide upon, revise and rationally pursue a conception of the good (Rawls 1980: 525; 1982: 164–5). Accordingly, Rawls declares that the nature of primary goods does not depend on 'historical or social facts'. The determination of primary goods requires a knowledge of the general circumstances and requirements of social life, but it does so 'only in the light of a conception of the person given in advance', a political conception of the person (Rawls 1985: 166; Rawls 1993: 75–6).

But, returning to the intergenerational context, what is this conception of the person if not a very specific one? Instead of admitting that primary goods are a function of a specific temporal and social environment, Rawls defines the primary goods as deriving from a concept of a person, which is, ultimately, once again, a function of a specific temporal and social environment. As Rorty (1988: 260) claims, 'the only theory of person we get is a sociological description of the inhabitants of contemporary liberal democracies'. And it may be, as some have warned us, that because of the need for drastic environmental policies in the future, the individualistic conception of society and the person will lose its popularity, to be replaced by a more totalitarian approach (cf. Ophuls 1977). Consequently, the contractarian cannot use the concept of primary goods in the intergenerational context because he cannot show that the conception of primary goods he has put forward will be appropriate to the circumstances of future life; or in terms of Rawls's more recent hypothesis, he cannot show that the conception of the person he has put forward will be appropriate to the circumstances of future life.

The assumption of a psychological motivation and other possibilities

However, there is an even more serious difficulty with regard to the impartial contractarian theory. It all starts with the assumption of a motivation: the people in the original position are not supposed to have obligations and duties to third parties, and the aim of justice as fairness is to derive all duties and obligations from other conditions. Thus Rawls introduces the assumption of a psychological motivation to explain the process of taking upon ourselves obligations to future generations. The parties in the original position

> are thought of as representing continuing lines of claims, as being so to speak deputies for a kind of everlasting moral agent or institution. They need not take into account its entire life span in perpetuity, but their goodwill stretches over at least two generations. . .. We may think of the parties as heads of families, and therefore as having a desire to further the welfare of their nearest descendants.
>
> (Rawls 1973: 128)

Does Rawls have any other alternative? Why does he choose to bring in the motivation assumption? Since the contractarian regards justice as having priority over other values, he cannot base obligations to future generations on other values or put them in a different context of discussion. For example, had he not seen justice as prior, he could have regarded obligations to future generations as being based on a duty to help the vulnerable (Goodin 1985, 1992b) or on some idea of the good, thereby obviating the need for a motivation. But this, of course, is in opposition to the entire tenor of Rawls's work and the contract theory: i.e. the priority of the right over the good.

Rawls sees a need for a motivation. After all, this is different from justice within a single generation, and one wonders what causes the people in the original position to concede many material benefits for the sake of people whom they might never know or see. Indeed, Rawls thinks that he must introduce the motivation assumption because, since the people in the original position know that they are contemporaries, they might favour their own generation by refusing to make any sacrifices at all for their successors (Rawls 1973: 140). Moreover, after constructing principles that declare that inequality is allowed only if it is for the greatest benefit of the least advantaged (the difference principle), Rawls must explain why we are now asked to reduce the welfare of the least advantaged contemporaries for the sake of persons who are not yet born. This, according to Rawls, calls for a motivation assumption.

But why does he use the model of a family? Why does he have the psychological motivation? I suggest that this has to do with a deep intuition: i.e. Rawls, like many of us, feels that intergenerational

justice is related to a sense of continuity. But the impartial contractarian cannot relate intergenerational justice to the transgenerational community, since the idea of community requires not only
that we live in communities, but also that these communities should
be valuable. The impartial contractarian, on the other hand, claims
that what makes a society just is not the telos at which it aims, but
precisely its refusal to choose in advance among competing ends and
ideas of the good life. So Rawls looks for something close to a
community, yet at the same time different and compatible with
individualistic liberalism, and this he finds in the family. He then
projects a situation in which each one of us saves for his offspring.
This, of course, is not precise, since the whole generation, including
those who do not or do not wish to have children, ought to be
represented in any decision-making concerning principles or policy.
In any case, it is clear that the family is the nearest the contractarian
can allow himself to approach the concept of a community.[12] Rawls
assumes that the idea of 'family ties' does not imply the good life,
especially when it is represented as the psychological motivation of
caring for one's descendants.

But is this correct? Is it not letting the idea of the good life enter
through the back door? My view of the family in this context is that
it represents a particular idea of the good life. No one can claim that
everyone who enters into the original position possesses such
feelings towards his or her children. Consider, for example, the
ideology that youngsters should 'fight their way out' of situations
and manage alone, not to mention parents who neglect their children.
Rawls's assumption that those in the original position have this
psychological motivation is, after all, an expression of the way he
would want us to be (Rawls 1958: 170).[13]

In fact, this must be a concept of the good life. If, taking the parties
as heads of families, the result of the original position is to arrive at
the same principles as those which are chosen in the intragenerational
case, then there is no need for this assumption of a psychological
motivation. If, on the other hand, Rawls suspects that these principles
might be different, then it seems that some people in one generation
who are badly off save or sacrifice for the sake of the institution of
the family, and not merely, as Rawls puts it, for the sake of the
fulfilment of justice in the future. Thus the family emerges as a very
strong idea of the good. In any case, for consistency the contractarian
ought to have held to the idea of the participants as individuals. Does
the motivation assumption mean that from now on the participants

will only consider the interests of families and not those of individuals? Should we consider the least advantaged families? The answers are not very clear. Moreover, we suddenly have to face the question of distribution within the family as a separate issue (i.e. if we reject Rawls's assumption that justice is not a virtue in the family), whereas, when everyone was considered an individual *per se*, every act of distribution was considered as belonging to a single category, which was distribution in society.

If the contractarian allows the participants to represent the family, she should allow them to represent other institutions as well. Why shouldn't the parties represent nations, social clubs and so forth? But instead of giving us the justification for the priority of the family, we are offered the psychological assumption, which is what Barry describes as 'a conjurer putting a rabbit in a hat, taking it out again and expecting a round of applause' (Barry 1977a: 279). Rawls brings in a psychological assumption and takes it out as an obligation.

For these reasons, D. C. Hubin tries to show how a contractarian could get the same results without altering the principle of mutual disinterestedness.

> If we assume that it is a general psychological principle that people who have children see their children's well-being essential to their own, then they will represent the interests of their immediate descendants in the deliberations concerning the principles of justice ... It does not matter that the tie exists between a parent and his child. It is only required that members of this generation identify the interests of some member of a future generation with their own.
>
> (Hubin 1976: 76 and note)

But then, although the contractors are mutually disinterested, they are still presumed to have a psychological motivation, because the sentiments exist 'out there' in the real world. More or less everyone has them, and so we can regard them as premises. So Hubin refers to the motivation as an empirical universal fact. But while this *may* of course be true, it is not necessarily so, as we pointed out earlier. And who is to guarantee that future people will feel the same?

Furthermore, the obligations as now defined are not to future generations but rather to contemporaries with regard to posterity and the attitude of contemporaries to posterity. Indeed, one option that is open to the contractarian is to imagine contemporaries having obligations with respect to future people. That is to say that the obligations which contemporaries have are to each other rather than directly to future people. But to argue that obligations to contemporaries with respect to future people exist is to make a far weaker claim than to claim obligations *to* future people, because the question of the objects of obligations (to whom do we owe *x*?) is no less important than that of the content of obligations (what do we owe?).

To illustrate this point, let us imagine the following scenario: suppose we have obligation Y to our contemporaries – say, an obligation to supply cheap rather than expensive energy. Later, we declare we have obligation Z, which is an obligation to contemporaries which is also relevant to the welfare of future people – for instance, not to store nuclear waste in the sea without being absolutely certain that it will never leak. Two years later we realize that the cheapest form of energy is nuclear energy and the cheapest way of eliminating the waste is by storing it in the sea. This means that obligations Y and Z contradict each other. 'No problem,' we say, 'Obligation Y has the priority' (let us assume that sea storage is absolutely safe during our lifetime). And we conclude, 'so let us forget about obligation Z'. Thus cheap energy continues to be supplied and nuclear energy waste is stored in the sea.

This arrangement seems morally plausible when both obligations are to contemporaries. But it is implausible to argue that obligation Y has priority when obligation Z is owed directly to future people, because the question arises: according to whose interests does it have priority? For future people obligation Z is at least as important as obligation Y because the radioactive waste might leak in *their* lifetime. Unless a good reason is given why contemporaries count more than future people, obligations to contemporaries in respect of future people are different from obligations that are owed directly to future people. So in the end, when Hubin has completed his argument, he arrives at an even weaker principle than Rawls does, and is still far from strengthening the case of contractarian theory.

To sum up so far, the motivation assumption which Rawls offers is problematic: it brings in the idea of the good life through the back door; it is contrary to the assumption of mutual disinterestedness; it is not necessarily empirically true; and it raises questions of justice within the family. By now it must surely be clear that there are so many difficulties associated with the assumption of a motivation that it is not worth pursuing. Still, Rawls's way forward may be to rely upon the motivation to be found in the original 'original position': the motivation to adopt the original position is to be just in accordance with the concept of 'justice as impartiality', and the motivation for the original position, behind the veil of ignorance, is self-interest. The question, then, is who the parties in the original position are: contemporaries (regardless of which generations they belong to), all who have lived and will live, or all who have lived, will live, or might live.

Rawls introduced the psychological motivation assumption to avoid the necessity of extending the original position to all generations, because that would be 'stretching fantasy too far' (Rawls 1973: 139). But the difficulty contractarians might find here with regard to those in the original position is much more serious. Why is this question so crucial? Because the contractarian claims that what makes this theory acceptable and preferable to others is its 'fairness'. The original position and the way it is arrived at are extremely important for the notion of fairness. It is the way principles of justice are attained which persuades us to accept them. But, of course, one of the variables that make the original position a fair one is the question of who is to participate in it and who is to be excluded. Presumably, if women had been excluded from the original position one would consider it unfair because they would not have been given a just and equal chance to determine the principles by which society is to be conducted. If we were told that men had a psychological motivation to consider the interests of women, we would perhaps be less critical; nevertheless, I believe that we would still have a very strong case against such an original position. The same applies to our case: we need a very good reason to explain why some future people are excluded from the original position when we consider future generations and intergenerational justice.

One way to avoid unfairness is to allow only contemporaries to enter the original position, but at the same time to extend the veil of ignorance to include information about the place of the generation in relation to other generations. That is to say, those involved would not know whether their generation is the first in history, the second, the twenty-seventh, or what else. But if we did so, those in the original position would follow a dominant strategy: a no-saving policy. Whether or not previous generations had saved (in the original positions this is not known), it would be better for contemporaries not to save, so an anti-environmental (no-saving, no-conservation) policy would be chosen.

Two scholars, however, recommend abandoning the psychological assumption and the present-time entry (the idea of entering the original position at the present time), and instead propose allowing all generations to participate. Jane English suggests doing this by opening the original position to all persons 'through history' (English 1977). Instead of searching for an additional saving principle, she argues, the difference principle itself is applicable to the context of intergenerational savings.

There are two possible cases in which the difference principle implies saving, she argues. The first case is when the level of welfare in a society is declining (we can think of the degradation of the environment). The difference principle would no doubt recommend saving for the sake of the least advantaged, who are the least advantaged of future generations. English is right, of course, in claiming that in cases of regress the difference principle may be sufficient to guarantee the approval of a saving principle; nevertheless, this is a wrong reading of the idea of savings and obligations to future generations, and represents a reduction of our obligations to *all* future people and to future generations (as collective entities) to partial obligations to parts of future generations, i.e. to the most needy among them. For instance our obligation to refrain from pollution (irrespective of progress or regress) applies to all future people and not merely to the least advantaged.

The second case is when society is in a state of progress. When contemporaries raise the level of the least advantaged and several alternative arrangements are possible, English argues, they should choose a policy that gives the highest level to the second worst off, and so on. The rationale, she argues, is that there are always, in times of progress, people in generation $n + 1$ that are in a lower position than people in generation n. What we need, then, is a technique that will help the best off in generation n to save for the sake of the worst off in generation $n + 1$, without lowering the position of the worst off in generation n. This, claims English, applies in cases when further help to the least advantaged (say by taxation) would 'destroy incentives and so operate to the disadvantage of everyone in this generation' (English 1977: 101), whereas incentives would not be harmed if the best off in the present were asked to invest some of their capital for the benefit of the least advantaged in future generations, e.g. in medical research. But here English comes up against the motivation problem again. She must show that the rich have a motivation to invest in a project that will bear fruit only a generation or more in the future. These better-off people could raise the level of the worst off of their generation even further if they wanted to, but they do not. Their excuse is that raising the level of the contemporary least advantaged even further would 'destroy incentives'. So why on earth would they want to invest for the sake of future people?

D. A. J. Richards (1983) also argues that the assumption of a motivation is in no way relevant to the original position. But from the impartial contractarian point of view one's actual generation is also irrelevant and should be kept behind the veil of ignorance, in exactly the same way as one's beliefs, race, nationality, etc. And the natural contractarian expression of this Kantian thought is to envisage a hypothetical contract including *all* generations. By this Richards means all people who exist, have existed, and will exist. Notice that in such a case one's desire to exist does not play a role, because everyone in the original position knows that he or she will live some time. People are therefore only concerned with ensuring that their existence will be as satisfying as possible (cf. Richards 1971: 134).

But this model poses its own difficulty: those in the original position are representatives of all persons throughout history; but who exactly are those 'persons throughout history'? Surely they include those who will be on earth one, two, or many generations from now. But are they the only ones who should be added to the expanded original position? Remember that we must construct the original position as fairly as possible. To see that there is a problem here, consider the following scenario. Suppose my wife and I are planning our future life. The question is whether to live in wealth and prosperity, spend a great deal of money on larger cars, fancy clothes, etc., and conceive only once; or to live a much more modest life, but have four children. Suppose, further, that the four 'candidates' for children exist somewhere in a different world and have the ability to communicate with us.

Now imagine that we have an original position in which we decide upon our policies. Since our policies will affect the candidates, we think it fair to consult them, or to let them participate in the original position. But it would be unfair to communicate only with the candidates who will later be conceived. If we haven't yet decided upon a policy, we should adopt a neutral position between all of them. The others should be given a chance to be heard, because if we decide upon another policy, one or more of them is going to be conceived. This thought-experiment illustrates the absurdity of the application of the idea of the original position and contractarianism to the intergenerational context. For how can we at one and the same time choose policies that will affect the identity of the people who will live, and ask the not-yet-born to join us in taking these decisions?

Suppose then that we let in all who live, will live, or might live if we changed our policies. Alas, in that case we can never reach an agreement upon a saving principle! Remember that no one knows which generation she belongs to, or whether she is someone who lives, will live, or might live if the policy were changed. We also assume that it is better to live than not to live. According to the maximin strategy, we are guided by our will to avoid a 'catastrophe', which in this case means not to be conceived at all. (Notice the difference with Richards's argument, where only those who lived and will live are represented. Then everyone knows he or she will live sometime, so the 'catastrophe' is not a matter of existence but rather of distribution.) Now all participants know that a policy X, of 'saving', or 'conservation', will cause some participants to live and others not to. On the other hand, if we do not adopt a policy of saving (policy Y), there will be others who will live. In that case they already do not know what to decide; the veil of ignorance must not allow them to know whether they will live or not. Their chances of living according to one policy or according to the other are not known to them. So how, according to the maximin strategy and following self-interest, are they to decide between these policies?

In short, the idea of a contract of representatives of all generations including those who might exist leaves us puzzled.[14] Moreover, there is no sense in talking about improving the welfare of the least advantaged resulting from different policies, since different policies will also produce different future people. Let me make it quite clear: it is neither because we harm potential people, nor because of their rights, that I find the concept of the original position problematic in the intergenerational context. Rather, it is because the salient feature of the original position is its fairness, and thus one cannot accept both a claim of fairness and such discrimination against those who would have lived had we chosen different policies.

5

RIGHTS OF FUTURE PEOPLE

Industrial man in the world today is like a bull in a china shop, with the single difference that a bull with half the information about the properties of china that we have about ecosystems would probably try to adapt its behaviour to the environment.
Teddy Goldsmith, *Ecologist* 1972

INTRODUCTION

The contractarian and the rights theories are not exclusive. One may hold both premises at one and the same time (Dworkin 1977; 1985). Rights theorists who are not contractarian may find that they still face difficulties quite similar to the ones that contractarians face in the context of intergenerational justice. Thus, some of our observations with regard to the contractarian theory apply to this chapter as well. But there are also some points which need to be raised specifically in connection with the rights-based theory and the concept of the rights of the not-yet-born.[1] My contention is that even if we attribute rights to future people – whether these are human or welfare rights – we are still left with serious and unresolved questions regarding the distribution of goods between contemporaries and future people according to the criterion of rights or, in other words, basing environmental policies on the rights of future people. Of course one may claim that future people do not have rights and still put forward an argument in favour of considering future generations when distributing goods, just as it is arguable that we should stop hunting without basing this claim on the rights of individual animals or of species. Indeed De George (1979), DeLattre (1972), Macklin (1981), and Steiner (1983) do precisely this. They all argue that there are constraints upon what contemporary people may do in matters affecting future people, but deny that these constraints have to do with the rights of future people. But others have argued forcefully in favour of the rights of future generations.

THE CONTROVERSIAL QUESTION OF THE RIGHTS OF FUTURE PEOPLE

The usual context envisaged in a discussion of rights is that of persons, or sometimes 'artificial persons', e.g. corporations (Raz 1986: 166). When we mention the right to free speech, the right to strike, and so forth, we are referring to human beings and in particular to adults. On the other hand, there are objects to which one can hardly, if at all, predicate rights: my bicycle is one example, your walking-shoes are another. However, there are some borderline cases which have been the focus of debate for quite a few years. These include, among others, animals, foetuses, and even children.[2] Future generations constitute a novel borderline case.

There are those who contend that one can certainly attribute rights to future people. Annette Baier, for example, denies the inferiority of the ontological status of future generations, claiming that the only special feature in a moral tie between us and future generations lies in the inferiority of our knowledge about them (A. Baier 1981: 174). A more positive argument is put forward by G. K. Pletcher, who describes a parallel case:

> If I have been camping at a site for several days, it is common to say that I have an obligation to clean up the site (. . .) for the next person who camps there.
>
> (Pletcher 1980: 168)

But Pletcher fails to see that this example is not parallel to the case of intergenerational relations, in that the persons who will use this camping site already exist at the time he cleans it up. It is only their future acts that are not yet conceived. Thus his obligations in this case parallel any other obligations he may have to people of his own generation whom he does not know personally.

Alas, the opposite view, according to which future people cannot be said to have rights, is also problematic. This position is taken, for instance, by Steiner, who argues that future people cannot be said to have moral rights because they cannot exercise the kind of choices that rights entail. To this Goodin very properly replies that he sees 'nothing in Steiner's argument logically disqualifying future generations from having rights. After all, court-appointed guardians exercise the rights of infants and idiots even though these are just as incapable as future generations of exercising choices themselves' (Goodin 1985: 179 fn 36). Richard De George also denies rights to future people:

> Future generations by definition do not now exist. They cannot now, therefore, be the present bearer or subject of anything, including rights. Hence they cannot be said to have rights in the same sense that presently existing entities can be said to have them. This follows from the briefest analysis of the present tense form of the verb 'to have'.
>
> (De George 1979: 95)

But this argument is not strong enough to disprove the idea that future people, *if and when* they exist, will have rights. What matters in this case is not that future people do not exist *now*, but rather that if and when they exist, future people will have rights. If so we should conserve the rain forests, clean up the beaches, reduce the use of gases which cause the greenhouse effect and so on, in order not to violate these eventual rights. This contention leads us to a third approach to our question, advanced by Joel Feinberg and Robert Elliot separately.

Those who have rights, argues Feinberg, are those who have (or can have) their own interests, often expressed as claims. He offers two reasons for this:

> (1) Because a right holder must be capable of being represented and it is impossible to represent a being that has no interests, and (2) because a right holder must be capable of being a beneficiary in his own person, and a being without interests is a being that is incapable of being harmed or benefitted, having no good or 'sake' of its own. Thus, a being without interests has no 'behalf' to act in, and no 'sake' to act for.
>
> (Feinberg 1980a: 167)

A being with interests should be distinguished from objects like rocks, or from monuments such as the Taj Mahal, which we treat respectfully although not for their own sake because they have no intrinsic value. So having interests is a status defined as 'being intrinsically valuable, i.e. being valuable independently of one's instrumental value.' (Raz 1986: 177).

So far so good. But on the one hand this becomes problematic because it is difficult to deny that there are some interests, at present existing, that future generations, at present non-existent, now have. For instance, future people have an interest in not being left an environment full of chemical pollution, e.g. toxic gases that are likely to disrupt the development of foetuses and cause birth defects. On the other hand, if there are such interests, then every potential man and woman has an interest to be born. Of course, even if we wanted to respect such an interest or such a right, we could not: acting in the name of the rights of future persons could justify environmental policies, but also the worst Malthusian scenario. In that case, can we really speak of future people's rights that exist *now*?

Once again, we encounter a significant difficulty. Imagine that all the inhabitants of our planet decide together that they no longer wish to reproduce, no woman conceives, and there are no future generations. One unwelcome result of this scenario would be that this book would no longer have any value. But, more relevantly, it seems that it would be a shame. Nevertheless, the rights theorist is silent about this outcome: since none of the rights of future people are being violated by such a decision – their existence being a prerequisite for their having rights – the proponents of the rights theory cannot condemn the earth's inhabitants for this unfortunate decision. If there are no interests now, how can we say that future people have claims? Moreover, does the fact that contemporary people are already alive whereas future people must first live before they are entitled to rights lead us again to the priority of contemporaries? (cf. Callahan 1981).

The answer to this question that has generally been put forward by rights-theory advocates is a claim of a 'potential interest': the rights that future people enjoy *vis-à-vis* contemporaries are, as Feinberg and Elliot describe it, 'contingent upon' the existence of future people. These are the interests that they are sure to have when they come into being; their identity is now obscure, but the fact of their interest-ownership when they do eventually come to exist is obvious.

The rights theorist can find help in the following. It may be that I have an interest in z although I have no right to it. For example, it may be in my interest, as indeed it is, to be bigger or taller, because I like playing basketball and I wish to play much better than I do. Nevertheless, I cannot claim to have a right to be taller. Thus, the conclusion that having an interest automatically implies having a right is far too presumptuous. But we could distinguish here between having an interest in the sense of having a desire which is congruent with other desires of mine, and having an interest which is something which can contribute to my well-being.[3] Environmentalists often find help in this distinction. For instance, Paul Taylor is probably referring to the second interpretation when he argues that 'once we come to understand [a butterfly's] life cycle and know the environmental conditions it needs to survive in a healthy state, we have no difficulty in speaking about what is beneficial to it and what might be harmful to it' (Taylor 1986: 66). But this applies to future generations as well. In the first sense, future people must first exist in order to have – or express – any wish or interest. Their first interest is therefore to exist, which – as I have argued – is unacceptable. But, in the second sense, future people do not need personally to wish or express their wishes, and thus it can be said that they have these interests when they exist without even having an interest in existence. In this second sense, future generations have an interest in a good, clean, healthy, environment.

So now we can assert that, with this interpretation of interests in mind, Elliot (1989) definitely concluded this phase of the debate when he suggested that the present non-existence of future people should not preclude our basing obligations to future generations on rights which they have or might come to have, and that future people can have 'contingent' rights and that 'the interests of future people generate obligations which are binding on us now'.

HUMAN RIGHTS

But what precisely do the rights of future people oblige us to do? Can the rights theorist answer this question? Some people see the essence of rights in their protection of individuals against interference by other individuals, institutions, or the state, in the preservation of their autonomous lives. These rights are sometimes termed 'human rights', as distinct from 'welfare rights', which are those rights which assume the state's intervention. But human rights are occasionally given a more 'activist' interpretation.

Henry Shue (1980) maintains that among the rights that should receive priority in the foreign policy of the United States are economic rights, which he calls 'subsistence rights'. If physical security is a basic right, he argues, then other aspects of security, e.g. minimal economic security, should be basic rights as well. Yet minimal economic security includes, according to Shue, not only adequate food, clothing and shelter, and preventive health care, but also unpolluted air, unpolluted water, and other environmental goods.

Some economists object to Shue's broad definition of rights, especially in the context of intergenerational justice. Their argument runs along the following lines.

(a) These rights should be enjoyed both by contemporaries and by future people.
(b) The practical consequence of, for instance, everyone enjoying adequate nutrition in the present is a population explosion. This makes the fulfilment of subsistence rights in the future impracticable, because it hurts the future poor and so the larger future populations will suffer from poorer nutrition.
(c) Thus, subsistence rights should be annulled in the present if they result in excessive population (cf. Hardin 1977).

Environmentalists and Green activists often argue by way of an answer that there are other ways of avoiding future famine: better allocation of the means of production, including knowledge, is one. In addition, I believe that the common view that economic prosperity inevitably leads to a population explosion is wrong. On the contrary, a higher standard of living and education tends to ensure the success of birth control programmes. It is the poor who usually have many children, e.g. in India, whereas the well-off and/or educated families tend to have fewer children. Besides, those who are worried about future people's rights should not seek the elimination of those rights in our own time.

James Sterba also offers a broad interpretation of the right to life, an interpretation which, he believes, will justify maintaining obligations to future people. The right to life implies not only that living persons should not be killed, but also that people should receive all the goods and resources necessary to satisfy their basic needs. Now, if future people are those we can definitely expect to come into existence, then:

> [A] right to life applied to future generations would be a right of a person whom we can definitely expect to exist to receive the goods and resources necessary to satisfy their basic needs or to noninterference with their attempts to acquire the goods and resources necessary to satisfy their basic needs.
>
> (Sterba 1981: 107)[4]

On the surface, this seems to mean that, if future people can be said to have rights, then one can find the moral grounds for our obligations to future people in the human rights of future people. But there are difficulties here. The first lies in the extent to which human rights, even as interpreted by Shue or Sterba, can justify the policies of provision to future generations that we intuitively feel we should follow. For example, one can justify a policy aiming at preventing hunger by an argument based on human rights; in that sense, human rights are related to redistribution. But one cannot justify redistribution of goods between two persons who are well above the poverty line by referring to the human right of satiety. Suppose, for instance, that there are two rich couples, Liz and John, and Robert and Carol. Liz and John, who have no children, earn more than Robert and Carol, who do have children. If the former are taxed in order that the state should supply the latter with child benefits, no human right of eliminating hunger or providing a greater or lesser degree of basic needs can be invoked in order to justify the policy. Analogously, our intuitions are that we have obligations to future generations that go beyond the obligations that derive from human rights. When we discuss matters of intergenerational justice we think of the distribution of products which include even non-essential goods, such as access to the enjoyment of aesthetically pleasing landscapes. The notion of human rights does not go far enough, and thus does not help in this discussion.

The second difficulty is that these interpretations of the rights of future people apply especially to purely material transfers from one generation to succeeding generations. Since we cannot store up bread and milk, simply because they will not be fresh enough in four generations' time, we put aside information, knowledge, and capital for the benefit of future generations. But what about obligations that have more to do with the environment? Should we leave rare species of animals in the world and refrain from harming lakes and forests because the human rights of future people require that we do so? Should we stop polluting the beaches of the Mediterranean because future people have the human right to sunbathe on clean sands? Can we even discuss such obligations in terms of human rights? I believe that we cannot, because the issue raised by these questions is economic progress, prosperity, and more jobs for contemporaries on the one hand, and a clean environment (for future people) on the other. The issue, then, involves not only weighing the claims of contemporaries against those of future people, but also evaluating two different goals for society, namely material progress versus conservation. Now, liberal scholars often claim that a theory of rights, as Dworkin has argued, is characterized by the idea that the most fundamental human right, from which all others derive, is the right to equal respect and concern. This right rests on the assumption of neutrality, which is the core of liberalism,[5] in that it reflects the importance ascribed to autonomy: people choosing for themselves from among a variety of ideas of what is good and planning their lives and developing themselves in the direction that they have chosen. This implies that the state should not promote any idea of the good life.

But when we decide to conserve, say, the Forest of Dean in England, it is because we think that forests are good, that activities such as walking in the woods are beneficial for people, and that they might be even more important than a hundred new jobs that could be created by building a Toyota car factory there. Therefore obligations to future generations related to the conservation of the environment cannot be based on the human right of equal concern in its liberal interpretation as a right that reflects neutrality.[6]

WELFARE RIGHTS

Because of all these difficulties, some people would suggest that the rights theorist should discuss the welfare rights of future people rather than their human rights.

What can the welfare rights of future people be? There are several definitions of welfare rights, some of which are so broad that they fail to help us in our discussion. In general, welfare rights are rights to a provision of services – and sometimes a minimal income – by the state, a firm, and so forth. The question that arises is what these services are. In Western social democratic states these include free or subsidized education, a health service, and unemployment benefits. These services vary from one society to another: public health, public transportation, higher education, and housing projects are included in the welfare services of some but not all societies. Thus it is often said that a minimal and yet a universal and acceptable definition of welfare is that which has to do with what we cannot do without (Goodin 1988).

Going back to the intergenerational context, the rights theorist faces a difficulty at this point. Since the standard of living has been rising, and since there is good reason to believe that it will continue to rise (although not, perhaps, at the same rate), what it is now reasonable to do without may at some future time be considered something that one cannot do without.[7] Does this imply that we should now supply future generations with all the welfare claims predicted for them? Supposing that these claims are higher than the claims of contemporaries; why should we supply these goods to future people and not to contemporaries, if we supply them at all? Is it merely because contemporaries have more modest expectations?

Moreover, the main difficulty with the theory of welfare rights of future generations lies in the derivation of a welfare right. How does one justify the claim that the state should subsidize one's medical treatment or that one's employer ought to pay one's pension? Unlike human rights – which are basically meant to prevent institutions or other individuals from interfering in individuals' lives – welfare rights cannot be based on individuals in the abstract. They must be based, rather, on individuals in their social contexts because, contrary to human rights, welfare rights inevitably emphasize one's social relations and are usually mentioned in the context of people who stand in an 'institutional relationship' and share a 'common institutional life' (Richards 1980: 469).[8] In other words, these rights – and, indeed, the provision of goods and services in general – have to do with membership and with obligations that we have to each other as members of the same community. If this is true, it has a far-reaching significance for our discussion of the rights of future people. However, let me first examine this argument and the criticisms against it.

Robert Goodin (1988) disagrees with the claim that welfare rights concern membership, distinguishing two possible arguments: that analytically and logically welfare rights derive from community, and that this is empirically true. He argues that although in the former instance this may usually be the case, it is nevertheless not enough to prove the assertion, and in the latter instance one should consider the other face of this argument, namely that non-members do not have welfare rights. This, he says, is false.

Goodin cites the example of many European countries that in the past granted women and children 'proto welfare' rights even though they were not at that time considered citizens in the sense of being people enjoying legal equality. But this does not prove Goodin's argument, because these women and children were given 'proto welfare' rights precisely because they were considered part of the community; legal citizenship, at that time, was possessed by very few, and was not equivalent to membership. For instance, in the Middle Ages the community embraced many people although very few had what we now call legal citizenship rights.

Goodin's second example is of residents who are not citizens and yet receive some welfare services, such as foreign workers in many countries. But this too fails to support his argument. On the contrary, it shows that, although citizenship is a common way of demonstrating membership (of the political community), one can still become a member of a community (which is not necessarily identical with the state) without being a citizen. Moreover, the policy of allowing foreign workers, for instance, to enjoy welfare benefits irritates some people – mainly those to the right of centre on the political map – because they fear that this constitutes the state's *de facto* recognition of these workers as new members of the community, and that formal citizenship is the natural next step.

Goodin's final example – that at one time travellers in Britain who were taken ill were treated free of charge – proves that receipt of health services does not indicate membership; however, it fails to prove that non-membership does not preclude the possession of welfare *rights* – as opposed to the enjoyment of some welfare or health *services*. Moreover, the case of health treatment for tourists in Great Britain is a special one that could be explained by Britain's desire to welcome tourists, or by the noble principle that a host is responsible for the health of his or her guests. These travellers were not entitled to any other welfare services (e.g. social security, unemployment benefits, etc.), and they did not and should not have interpreted the generosity of the British government and people as an expression of their 'welfare rights'. In addition, the fact that this norm changed and the regulation was cancelled without international protest indicates that nobody considered this treatment as a welfare right.

In general, welfare rights make sense only in the context of a community. As long as political communities such as the state exist, it is difficult to accept, for example, that a Frenchman can claim a welfare right from Mexico. As Michael Walzer argues, claims to welfare rights are claims depending on the character of a particular political community, and they are fixed only when a community adopts some programme of general provision. Distributive justice in the sphere of welfare refers to the recognition of need, but also to the recognition of membership (Walzer 1985: 78). Thus, if welfare rights are community based, the advocates of the welfare rights of future people cannot premise their theory on the notion of rights. Welfare rights in that sense are no longer primary, because they derive from our understanding of a community, and in our context the transgenerational community. We therefore return to the question of whether future people share with contemporaries some kind of transgenerational community.

But, you may ask, how can it be argued that the community is the fundamental concept when in modern liberal societies individualism is dominant? This individualism is so deeply rooted that some philosophers have challenged the very possibility of environmental ethics, if the agent in the environmental discourse is species or ecosystems rather than individuals (Thompson 1990: 154). But notice that although liberal individualism is both a methodology and a normative stand (Avineri and de-Shalit 1992: Introduction), some people fail to reflect on individualism when it comes into conflict with new elements, such as ecology. Instead of re-evaluating their form of individualism *vis à vis* the new information or new philosophical arguments, they make individualism into a sacred truth. Interestingly, several recent papers have discussed these matters. One paper showed that the American ethos of individualism influenced environmental legislation in the United States so that individual animals are protected in the country, whereas in Europe environmental legislation emphasizes the community which includes nature (Rothenberg 1992), and another work claimed that 'volitional interdependence' should replace free will as the correct principle in an understanding of the relationship of nature, culture, and agency (Murphy 1992). This leads us to my final comments on the individualistic theories versus the communitarian theory of intergenerational justice.

6

SUMMARY AND OPEN QUESTIONS

Farmers today are very clever; with the help of the Government and the Common Market, they continue to make a great deal of money from what they do. But they are not wise, for they are serving their own interests only by working against the interests of the land.

Jonathon Porritt *Seeing Green*

NOTES ON THE COMMUNITARIAN THEORY OF INTERGENERATIONAL JUSTICE

Before I sum up my argument, I would like to make six comments on the communitarian theory of intergenerational justice *vis à vis* the theories which I have criticized.

1   *The communitarian theory of intergenerational justice locates the source of our obligations to future generations in ourselves and takes full responsibility for the state of the environment.*   When the utilitarian, contractarian, and rights-based theories of intergenerational justice were discussed, indicating the pitfalls encountered by such theories, I noted that we need a theory that would establish the grounds for our obligations to future generations in the needs and duties of contemporaries rather than, for instance, in the rights of future people.

First, it is a matter of who takes the responsibility for the environment that we leave to future generations. The three theories criticized – especially the contractarian one – fail to do this.

In order to avoid the difficulty of not being able to know what future people will agree upon, the contractarian theorists introduce the idea of reiterating a contract between three generations that live

123

at the same time (Gauthier), or the idea of representing the interests of future generations through the interests of contemporary 'heads of families' (Rawls). But there are acts of ours that affect only the more remote future generations, leaving the more immediate future generations unaffected (sometimes these are called 'time bombs'). In addition, many environmental policies involve planning for a very long period ahead. We should therefore not reduce the question of intergenerational justice to relations between one generation and its direct successor. If, for instance, we fail to store waste correctly – say, by not paying attention to the material the storage apparatus is made of – then we are in danger of acting immorally. A theory must therefore provide us with a justification for such obligations; all that contract theories do, however, is hope that the obligation which contemporaries have to the succeeding generation will be passed on from that generation to the next and so on. This is not enough, for it might be interpreted in a way that demands no effort of the first generation: it might store the nuclear waste in a way that ensures that no leakage occurs for only two generations, trusting the next generation to ensure by its own means that there is no leakage in the more distant future, and so on. This is too risky a policy, for what will happen if the next generation does not find a way to ensure the prevention of radioactive leakage?

Now the communitarian theory of intergenerational justice is a theory which relies on contemporaries to do the entire job. It is based on a conception of the self in which its existence is not absolutely limited in time. Without entering into mystical concepts of eternal existence (life after death),[1] our theory follows another model in which the self is not totally confined within the barriers of its own physical existence. In this theory, one's self-awareness is related to one's community, both in the present and in the future, i.e. in relation to the aims, desires, ideas, dreams, and values of the transgenerational community. By extending the community to include future genera- tions, I have argued that obligations are owed directly to them, and that since these obligations derive from the community that consti- tutes our 'selves', contemporaries should take these obligations very seriously, as they indeed have good reason to do.

2   *The communitarian theory releases us from dependence on impossible information and does not pretend or aim to be neutral.*
The theories which I have criticized fail to deal with the existence of ideas of the good and their relevance in the intergenerational context,

either because they need but cannot have information about what constitutes the good of future generations, or because in order to be consistent they must be neutral, which is impossible in the inter-generational context.

Suppose an idea or a project is important, meaningful, and significant to me. If it has a political character (e.g. if public money is needed to promote it), I shall introduce it as a general good, valuable for the whole society, because I regard politics as an arena for a debate in which one tries to convince others of one's ideas. Politics take place in the 'forum', to use Elster's expression (1986). In this forum you expect me to provide you with a rational argument for wanting you to act in a certain way, or for wanting the government to allocate resources to a certain group, and so forth. I imply, from the fact that something is subjectively significant, that it is significant and important for the whole of society. For example, if I prefer to live in a society in which people may be less affluent yet enjoy an environment free of pollution or with a high level of mental health, if I am troubled by the existence of animal abuse, or of much drug addiction, I assert that the government should allocate more money to environmental policies, health services, social work-ers, anti-drug campaigns, and so on. I am not content with declaring that it is my concern or interest, and that I personally would like to see fewer animal experiments because it irritates or frightens me, or whatever; I try to persuade others that what I believe is right and good. I therefore develop a strong and intense relationship towards the ideas I believe in, fight for, and so on. I regard them as part of me, of what I am.

The contractarian and rights-based theorists, on the other hand, do not accept this approach. They claim that if X is significant for person A, and Y is significant for person B, then society should remain neutral between the two. Instead of choosing one over the other (if they contradict one another), the two or more sides should compromise: in Elster's words, this is a market. Ideas are not part of us: they are not to be regarded as important elements of what we are. Rather they become objects that we own and 'trade' with as if they were goods external to ourselves.[2] A division is thus erected, not only between the two or more interacting persons, but also between the persons and their desires; a person should not regard the ideas as part of her, and in many cases she should even be prepared to give up the dream of living according to her ideas.

But can one 'alienate' oneself from one's attitudes and play a neutral role with regard to the future, or to objects that we think we should conserve for future generations – in fact, to conservation itself?

Dworkin, in an attempt to reconcile individualistic liberalism with conservation, contends that it is possible to argue for conservation in the name of neutrality between different ideas of the good. He writes:

> Suppose ... that the liberal holds a ... belief about the importance of preserving natural resources. He believes that the conquest of unspoiled terrain by the consumer economy is self-fueling and irreversible, and that this process will make a way of life that has been desired and found satisfying in the past unavailable to future generations, and indeed to the future of those who now seem unaware of its appeal. He fears that this way of life will become unknown, so that the process is *not neutral* amongst competing ideas of the good life, but in fact destructive of the very possibility of some of these.
>
> (Dworkin 1985: 202; emphasis added)

But this argument is simply wrong. If you tell me that you are going to choose between a number of ideas ranging from idea 1 to n minus 1 and I assert that you should choose between ideas ranging from 1 to n, you will ask me why I insist on n. My answer cannot be 'because it is there', because then you will ask 'well then, why not idea $n + 1$?' I must consequently explain that n is desirable, significant, important, or something of that nature, or else it does not make any sense. It is precisely because the object has been 'desired and found satisfying in the past' that we want future people to enjoy it. Moreover, we do not preserve what we think is bad, what we do not find satisfying; we sometimes even try to destroy it for the sake of posterity, e.g. nuclear weapons. According to Dworkin's argument we should conserve nuclear weapons – indeed, the idea of war itself – so that future generations will be aware of that demonic phenomenon and have the opportunity to choose between a variety of ideas of the good. In short, the argument that we should conserve an object for the sake of future generations must be based on a claim that this object is in itself good.[3] How in fact could we speak of inter-generational justice without having some notion of the good? For by deciding what future generations will need or want, and by distributing goods, we in fact predict and dictate what goods will be available in the world of the future, and what future lifestyles will be like. We thereby shape the patterns of future societies, and inevitably bring in the idea of the good. We cannot remain neutral conceiving conceptions of the good over long periods of time.

Or what if we decide that it is best to supply future generations with electricity, and consequently cut down all the trees in our area? Aren't we deciding for our posterity what is good (industrialized societies) and what is unnecessary (forests, nature)? One cannot avoid deciding when planning. But these theorists try to tackle the issue of intergenerational justice with the same assumptions and theories with which they discuss justice within a single generation. Precisely because the contractarians insist on respecting autonomy as a guiding principle, they then find out that they cannot know whose autonomy to respect, and thus fail to show respect for future people (not to mention non-human animals or nature) by pursuing and supporting environmental policies. Utilitarians, on the other hand, are not afraid of speaking in terms of the good, but they easily contradict their universalism and temporal principle of neutrality by imposing their own conception of the good on future generations.

But, according to the communitarian theory, the obligations that we have to future people and the policies adopted for their sake do not necessarily contradict obligations to contemporaries in all respects. Indeed, if we think of environmental policies, they are for the sake of posterity, but also for the sake of our contemporaries. We would like to improve the welfare of contemporaries, but this welfare is not only a matter of material resources; on the contrary, it also includes the quality of life. For instance, people care not only how many books they have on their shelves, but also what kind of books they have, and thus the kind of books people have is part of their welfare. In the same way, it is true, as some claim, that while we do not gain anything material by following a theory of intergenerational justice it does add relevance and meaning to our lives.

3   *The communitarian theory of intergenerational justice saves us from dependence on the ontological issue of potential versus actual persons.*   In the previous chapters we saw that other models of intergenerational justice lead to difficulties in identifying future people. With the communitarian model we can overcome this problem because there is no need to identify actual future people. Since the theory ties the obligations and their origin to us, the present generation, we need not calculate someone else's utilities, nor relate the obligations to the rights of someone else who is not yet alive in

order to find the moral grounds for our obligations to future generations. The assertion that we have obligations to future generations is separated from questions of population policies, the identity of future people, and so forth. Unlike the utilitarian, contractarian, and rights-based theories, the communitarian does not have to identify future people before constructing a theory of obligations towards them. We are left with questions which affect the content of our obligations to posterity, e.g. the size of future populations. These, however, are practical problems relating to the application of the theory, rather than problems of essence. They are concerned with determining the size of the pie and the extent of the resources that we need to set aside for future people, whereas the difficulties in the other theories arose from the necessity of justifying the obligations themselves.

4   *The communitarian theory has the advantage of not being atomistic.*   All three theories I have criticized regard individuals as prior to society. They hold that a person is a universal phenomenon that can be understood independently of the context of language, culture, history, and therefore time as well. The self is capable of definition without being related to society, customs, and norms. Instead the agents display what Gauthier calls 'non-tuism': namely, they are unconcerned with the interests of those with whom they interact. In the sphere of the environment this has unfortunate consequences, because each individual seeks to increase her utilities whereas she would like the others to seek the common good. But the tragedy is that if all the individuals seek their own self-interest, no one seeks the common good (in environmental ethics this is called 'the tragedy of the commons').

So we are asked to regard our society as an aggregation of individuals, and relations between the 'generations' should be understood in the same way. Hence these theories are 'atomistic'. Justice, then, is seen as a matter of relations between separate persons, 'resolving rival claims of discrete substantial beings' (Bickham 1981: 174). Alas, if relations among contemporaries are of this nature, so are the relations between contemporaries and future people. The environmentalist wishes to justify the concession of some material benefits, as well as an adjustment to co-operation. However, it is difficult, if it is possible at all, to base this on atomism and self-interest. Can co-operation with George who will live in the twenty-fifth century be in the economic self-interest of Ruth who lives in the twentieth century?

This difficulty is related to the concept of alienation, or perhaps to an extension of it. The individualist self, as represented in the three theories, is alienated in relation to the past and future, and thus to the environment, living only in the present. It has no sense of belonging to anything larger than its own private sphere, such as the human race, history, an ecosystem, nature, a national effort, a class struggle, a cultural transfer from one generation to another, or a creative multigenerational effort – all of which has been described as 'self-transcendence'.

5   *The communitarian theory of intergenerational justice is time-neutral.*   A further advantage of the communitarian theory is that it is also time-neutral: it seems reasonable enough for a future person to assert that we contemporaries should not discriminate against her when distributing goods simply on the grounds that she lives in a different time in the future and we live in the present (cf. de-George 1979). 'If that is so,' you may ask, 'how can you say that we have less intensive obligations to people who will live many generations from now?' But on a deeper examination of this question we see that the actual reason for less intensive obligations to very remote future generations is not the temporal distance of these generations but rather their being in a different (or almost different) community because there is not enough cultural interaction and moral similarity between us. Their distance from us in time adds another dimension to the transgenerational community, but it is not the reason for the so-called discrimination. However, let me remind the reader again, we do have some strong obligations which call for urgent policies even towards very remote future generations, but these obligations do not derive from communitarian relations.

6   *The communitarian theory of intergenerational justice is help-ful in identifying the content of our obligations to future genera-tions.*   We saw in previous chapters that the utilitarian and the contractarian approaches could not answer the question of the content of our obligations to future generations: 'Insofar as it is within our control, should we aim for our great grandchildren having whatever kind of world would seem to its inhabitants most satis-fying, or should we be guided by our own preferences?' (Glover 1979: 86). But if we follow the three theories I have described, how can we

know or predict what their tastes will be? How can we know if we should leave them green forests or industries?

The communitarian theory circumvents this problem; in fact, we need not know the preferences of future people at all, but, rather, can decide what to leave to future generations on the basis of our own values. Suppose, for example, that we decide not to touch picturesque towns and leave them as they are for future generations to enjoy. If it emerges that some future generation dislikes conservation and prefers rapid transportation and motorways crossing downtown, then it is very likely that, in any case, that generation does not share our values, and thus is not a part of our transgenerational community. Therefore our obligations to this future generation are in any event reduced (they consist of mainly 'negative' obligations) and we have not harmed that generation by leaving it beautiful monuments and narrow streets instead of huge cars, which is what it prefers.

At first sight the example of the city is vulnerable; you may argue that there is a realistic possibility that a future generation will dislike picturesque urban centres despite the fact that, roughly speaking, it will belong to our transgenerational community. However, the theory refers more generally to a *package* of objects that we leave to future people rather than to this or that single commodity. That is to say, we leave to future generations a package of natural resources, achievements in art and science, technology, knowledge, values, financial resources, and so forth on the assumption that they will want this package.

Thus, the communitarian model releases us from a difficult and problematic question, to which we have thus far found no answer in the other ethical theories. I should add that I do not claim to have found the precise formula for striking a balance between our obligations to future generations and improving the welfare of contemporaries. Nevertheless, I think that the communitarian theory of intergenerational justice indicates the direction we must take in order to discover this equilibrium.

Now, to what extent should we consider future generations when to do so contradicts improving the welfare of contemporaries? The answer, as I have argued, is partly a political one, and should be understood politically. The political theorist should therefore have something to say about this issue. In this sense, this book leaves some unfinished work. So let us very briefly raise the questions that remain to be discussed. They fall into three categories.

1 The economic question: What is the rate of progress or development that would both guarantee the fulfilment of obligations to
   future generations and improve the welfare of contemporaries?
2 The question concerning political science: what are the institutions
   and the economic and social system that can best tackle the issue
   of the environment?
3 The question concerning international relations: what is the relationship between the communitarian theory of intergenerational
   justice and the measures that have to be taken internationally in
   order to guarantee the fulfilment of our obligations to posterity?

With regard to the first question, there are three basic views of resources, growth, conservation, and progress (cf. Kahn 1977). At one extreme are the so-called 'dark Greens' or 'deep ecologists' and the 'neo-Malthusians'. They argue that the world is a finite pie, so what we exhaust is not available to future people and therefore, the more we deplete, the poorer they will be. If there are any techno-logical solutions to problems such as pollution, they are delusive. The most they can do is postpone the immediate need for drastic political or environmental action. This might prove disadvantageous, because such postponements will only cause mankind to remain apathetic instead of taking steps towards genuine solutions to the problems. Hence the extremists among them tend to idealize and pine for the pre-industrial societies, picturing a catastrophe for future people if we do not retreat from our present positions. However, most environmentalists do not go so far. For instance, Jonathon Porritt, the ex-director of Friends of the Earth, thinks that 'in no way do ecologists contemplate a return to the primitive deprivations and discomforts of the pre-industrial age' (Porritt 1984: 215), and Eugene Hargrove searches for a balanced value system (Hargrove 1988: 206–15).

At the other end of the scale stand the developers and the growth enthusiasts. The world, they say, is an unlimited pie, and global productivity must be raised rapidly in order to meet the challenge of feeding the growing population. They are not reluctant to utilize technology, capital, and science – including economics which, they say, can provide superb solutions to the problem of lack of resources such as pricing the environment, which limits the use of scarce resources. In fact, they claim, all problems are soluble, either by people or by technology, and if by neither then politics can easily arrange a solution (cf. Ehrenfeld 1978: 16–17). Science and industry are the means by which the Third World, or the underdeveloped countries, may overcome their economic difficulties and poverty and by which the least advantaged in every society will improve their positions. In any case, they claim, people like the way they live, and therefore future people will enjoy life even if they see fewer species of animal and smell a limited variety of flowers. Of course, this attitude completely neglects non-instrumental values in nature. But it is problematic in another sense. If it implies that when we dry up all lakes people will enjoy driving cars rather than sailing, so be it. But according to the same rationale we can limit to a minimum (say two) the variety of options people have for amusement and yet nobody will be hurt because 'they will learn to enjoy what they have'. This is absurd. So something different must be expressed by this claim, namely that, instead of sailing in natural lakes or canoeing in rivers, people will sail a gondola in an artificial lake and will think 'Boy, this is wild!' Such an attitude is wrong, because it takes wilderness to be relative, whereas in fact wilderness was here long before anything artificial existed and is in that sense absolute.[4]

But many people think that the truth lies somewhere in between. They reject theories of growth limits as well as traditional theories of progress. Some describe themselves as 'pale Greens': they think we should find a middle way between the two extremes, not only because this is a just way of considering this issue, but also because this is a realistic approach to the issue. Development provides the opportunity for creativity and improvement, but its other side must be conservation; technology is both good and evil; industry not only creates pollution but also makes possible the manufacture of medicine, means of transportation, and communication – all of which are necessary for running a democratic regime – and so forth. Progress may have engendered pollution and radioactivity, many people argue, but it was the only way employment could have been guaranteed. The art of managing the economy and the environment is the art of modifying and controlling industrial growth, while at the same time providing welfare, health care, education, and all the other requirements of modern society.

Many economists and politicians use the term 'sustainable development' to describe this attitude. For instance, in its Tokyo Declaration of 1987 the World Commission on the Environment and Development declared that the only way to build a future that would be prosperous, just, and secure would be by adopting the objective of 'sustainable' development, which was defined as 'an approach to progress which meets the needs of the present without compromising the ability of future generations to meet their own needs' (World Commission on the Environment and Development 1987: 363).

Sustainable development differs from economic growth: first, development is more than simply a rise in income or in gross national product. The emphasis is shifted from indicators of quantity to the 'quality of life' (hence the dropping of the term 'economic') and to moderate and responsible progress, which includes environmental factors (hence 'development' rather than 'growth'). Second, sustainable development takes into account the long-term effects of our policies and not only the short-term ones, and thus refers not only to the welfare of contemporaries and the younger generation but also to that of future people who are not yet born. Sustainable development, then, means that 'future generations must not inherit less environmental capital than the current generation inherited' (Pearce et al. 1989: 3). Of course 'environmental capital' can be interpreted to permit environmental losses to be offset by financial compensation or even better knowledge, technology, etc. But this is not to say that we can deplete the natural resources provided we leave enough capital for future generations. Sometimes, perhaps quite often, environmental wealth is no less important than capital. 'Whatever is done,' advocates of sustainable development say, 'it is important to remember that, at the present rate of consumption, some natural resources may be nearly exhausted by the end of the twenty-first century. We should not try to get round the problem by allowing ourselves to deplete resources and compensate future generations in terms of money, or even knowledge and technology. This mode of compensation may be acceptable, but only after other means, e.g. decreased production, re-use, or recycling, have been adopted.'

In that sense, the principle that determines our obligations to future generations as providing equal opportunities of access to resources is acceptable only as a very broad framework. This principle has been put forward by a number of scholars. The first was John Locke; following his description of the state of nature, Gregory Kavka (1978) argued that we should leave 'enough' to future people. Then Brian Barry (1979, 1983b) suggested a formula: the overall range of opportunities open to future generations should not be narrowed. Thus, for instance, if we burn 10 per cent of the oil, we should improve the technique of using solar energy by at least 10 per cent. But sustainable development implies that priority should be given to policies such as recycling over policies such as compensating environmental depletion with greater knowledge. At the same time, sustainable development does not imply that we contemporaries should cease economic development or industrialization.

The first question that remains to be discussed, then, is which one of the three approaches to progress or development would be likely to guarantee the fulfilment of our obligations to contemporaries and to future generations? The second question to be considered is, what sort of political and economic system is likely to guarantee the fulfilment of these obligations? Most of us agree that we have obligations to future generations. However, while some of us think that the best way to guarantee the fulfilment of these obligations is by a free market with a minimum of state intervention, others think that strong state intervention, a radical stagnation, and slowing down of the economy are required (cf. Seabrook 1990; Moberg 1991; Eckersley 1992).

According to the market model, all we have to do is value the environment and natural resources and their usage will automatically become more limited. The idea that we can put prices on commodities such as air is not entirely new. Surprisingly, J. S. Mill conceived such a possibility in the nineteenth century:

> Air, for example, though the most absolute of necessaries, bears no price in the market, because it can be obtained gratuitously: to accumulate a stock of it would yield no profit or advantage to anyone; and the laws of its production and distribution are the subject of a very different study from Political Economy.... It is possible to imagine circumstances in which air would be a part of wealth. If it became customary to sojourn long in places where the air does not naturally penetrate, as in diving bells sunk in the sea, a supply of air artificially furnished would, like water conveyed into houses, bear a price: and if from any revolution in nature the atmosphere became too scanty for the consumption, one might acquire a very high marketable value.
> (Mill 1900: 7)

Contemporary advocates of the market argue that just because we had always thought clean air was cheap, and was in fact a resource with a zero price, people polluted it without a second thought. Now we should understand that the environment has a positive economic value. Some Libertarians even claim that the scarcer the resource becomes the faster a market will be generated. But the economist David Pearce forcefully opposes this Libertarianism. He argues that it is not clear how many zero-priced resources could be subject to exclusive ownership, and that it is doubtful whether this market evolution would take place in time to prevent the extinction of those resources (Pearce *et al.* 1989: 26 fn 2). The problem is that, ultimately, the market ignores the needs of future people. First, although prices may be high, the market will still be free, with no official obstacles to the depletion of natural resources or the pollution of the clean environment. Since natural resources are consumed on a 'first come, first served' basis, contemporaries may be willing to pay a great deal and use these resources rather than trouble with conservation. Second, there are too many questions with no definite answer. Who will fix the prices? Who will pay whom? Will contemporaries pay other contemporaries or will they compensate future generations by paying to them? How will it be done? (cf. Anderson 1977). Therefore, critics of the market solution to environmental problems argue that managing the environment is a very complicated task. The market model, in fact, leaves this job to protest groups: but however vital they are, it is doubtful whether these groups could carry the burden alone. The state must take part and environmental issues must be solved by planning and the enforcement of laws and policies.

Market advocates respond that steps could always be taken after the problems are discovered or revealed; intervention is not necessary and should be limited. However, if we must intervene, we will. Besides, they claim, it is sometimes even better to postpone our reactions because better information will be available in the future. But their opponents argue that, since some delays may cause irreversible environmental damage (e.g. the destruction of species, 'holes' in the ozone layer, radioactive leakages), the market approach does not take obligations to future generations very seriously, and we should therefore adopt an 'anticipatory mode' of action.[5] Hence, the second issue to be discussed is whether free-market policies can guarantee the fulfilment of our obligations to future generations.

The third major issue to be tackled is, perhaps, the most urgent political task: the international aspect of the management of environmental problems. Economists distinguish between 'common property resources' and 'open access resources' (Pearce *et al.* 1989: 12). Some parts of the environment are 'common property resources', e.g. parts of the ocean that are open to a few nations' fleets. Both these kinds of resources in Pearce's words 'run the risk of over-use'. Global open access resources such as the atmosphere 'are very likely to be overused'. These are public goods; once they are provided to one person or nation they are provided to everyone and to all nations. Thus in addition to having a theory of intergenerational justice we must guarantee international co-operation as well. This includes fields such as the transportation of toxic materials, re-use and recycling, land use, urbanization, international evaluation of the potential impact of economic development and new technologies and industries, scientific research, population policies, and so on.

One of the most urgent issues is international agreements and their enforcement. The greatest problem is the 'veto state' – a state that attempts to weaken proposals for international co-operation on an environmental issue (Porter and Brown 1991: 104, table). For example, in 1986, forty years after the first International Convention for the Regulation of Whaling was signed – but never implemented – the International Whaling Commission banned all commercial whaling, but a veto coalition (Japan, Norway, Peru, and the USSR) employed an 'indirect strategy' (Porter and Brown 1991: 81) and switched to 'scientific' whaling. Another difficulty is the co-ordination of many national policies on greenhouse gas emissions, but the burden is not equally distributed: first within the affluent world (Holland's commitment is to a 5 percent annual reduction of CO_2 from the level of the year 1990 by the year 2000, whereas Japan is committed to the stabilization of all greenhouse gases at the level of the year 1990 by the year 2000) and second between the north and south.[6]

Indeed, the wealthier countries are today becoming increasingly 'green'; they tend to refrain (at least more than they used to) from polluting the rivers and lakes, or cutting down forests. But this is often at the cost of polluting and depleting the resources of the poorer countries of the Third World. These countries often 'export' land for storing toxic materials,[7] or sell their own wood and other natural resources. Sierra Leone has officially contracted with the United States to permit American firms to dump toxic wastes there. In 1980 Haiti signed several such contracts with other countries (Devos *et al.* 1986). According to the Pearce report, 80 per cent of the world market in tropical hardwood is supplied by five countries: Malaysia, Indonesia, the Philippines, the Ivory Coast, and Gabon. The five exporting countries need the money to improve the welfare of their citizens. Thus, they do not invest the money they get from export in reforestation (which would be for the benefit of future generations). This means that in fact the wealthy countries do not

follow a Green policy, nor do they care enough for future generations. It is here that international co-operation should be introduced;
at the very least, the matter should be discussed internationally and
with more success than in Rio in 1992. Perhaps the price of wood
should be raised, on condition that the increase in wealth that these
countries receive is devoted to reforestation.

It should be pointed out that theoretically it may not be very
difficult to establish international co-operation, since every person
belongs to several communities (e.g. a nation, a party, a religious sect,
a class, an ideological movement, etc.), of which many are international. Unfortunately, however, international co-operation is in
reality far from satisfactory, perhaps because the dominant community is that of the nation. This raises questions of international
intergenerational justice (obligations of a person in one community
to a future person in another community). I am aware of these
questions, but cannot consider them here. I therefore reiterate that
the issue of international co-operation is perhaps the first issue that
should be addressed once the moral grounds for our obligations to
future generations are established.

The communitarian theory of intergenerational justice suggests
that in each community people should decide on certain policies and
refrain from certain acts because they owe it to future generations.
But if the people of Holland, for instance, follow these policies and
the people of France do not, the policies of Holland will lose their
effectiveness. The same applies to damage to trees: it has been found
that sulphur dioxide and nitrogen dioxide, which 'travel' across
borders, damage the trees all over Europe and North America. The
third issue, then, is that of international co-operation and a world
'regime'.

These three issues and other questions remain to be tackled. However, my task is limited to the first part of the discussion, i.e. to
principles of distribution within a community of provision. Once we
have found the moral grounds for considering future generations in
the process of distribution, we will then be in a position to discuss
the means of guaranteeing the fulfilment of our obligations and forms
of international co-operation.

NOTES

INTRODUCTION

1 It is useful at this point to define the concepts of 'generation' and 'future generations'. A generation is a set of people who are of more or less the same age and who live at the same period in history, usually regarded as having a span of thirty years. Future generations are people who by definition will live after contemporary people are dead.

2 For an economic consideration of these issues, see Pearce *et al.* (1989); for a philosophical point of view see Brennan (1984), Goodpaster and Sayre (1979), Jonas (1984), and Taylor (1986).

3 Cf. Heyd (1988, 1992), Parfit (1984), and Sikora and Barry (1978).

4 This is thought to be the second most important political problem, before inflation, European unity, arms limitation and so on. Cf. DG Information, Communication and Culture, Brussels, Eurobarometer, No. 30, Dec. 1988. Reprinted in Pearce *et al.* (1989: xiii). For attitudes in Britain see O'riordan (1991) and Young (1990). For attitudes in the United States see Pollock *et al.* (1992).

5 The title of an influential book by Taylor (1986). Cf. Attfield (1987, 1991), Brennan (1988), Frankena (1974), Hargrove (1988), Rolston (1986, 1988, 1989), Wenz (1988), and Nash (1989). For two different views see Bernard Williams (1991) and Thomson (1992) who has doubted the value of discussing 'intrinsic good' in general.

6 For literature on our moral relationship with animals see Clark (1977), Feinberg (1980a), Rachels (1991), Regan (1982, 1983), Rollin (1981), Singer (1979), and Sprigge (1984).

1 THE TRANSGENERATIONAL COMMUNITY

1 The reader may refer to Avineri and de-Shalit (1992: Introduction) Gutmann (1985) or Sandel (1984a). For a discussion and assessment of some communitarian arguments see *Ethics*, vol. 99, July 1989: 695 ff.

2 Compare with Peter Singer's celebrated article (1972) about obligations to remote people.

3 Compare with Bob Goodin's claim (1992) that demanding too much in terms of personal life style was not a successful Green strategy.

4 This term refers to Robert Paehlke's interesting book (1989) and article (1990).

5 Aristotle, *The Politics*, 1967, New York: Penguin, 1253a1.

6 The idea that the basis for our treatment of one another – our having duties to other members of the community – lies in the actual existence of the community seems so self-evident that even some liberals accept it for some forms of community. As Dworkin writes: 'Political association, like family and friendship and other forms of association more local and intimate, is in itself pregnant of obligation' (Dworkin 1986: 206). The argument is even more popular among communitarians. In a similar vein to Dworkin, Michael Walzer considers obligations that derive from actual reciprocal relationships. 'Obligations', he writes, 'begin with membership,' and 'commitments to principles are usually also commitments to other men, from whom or with whom the principles have been learned and by whom they are enforced' (Walzer 1970a: 5, 7).

7 Some identify rationality with an impersonal, universal point of view; I certainly do not mean this, as it is doubtful whether this definition of rationality is at all compatible with the notion of community. I mean that behaviour is rational when (a) one can identify one's goals; and (b) one can identify the means of achieving these goals; and (c) one chooses what seems to be the best way to achieve the goals sought; and (d) if this turns out to be a bad choice, then one corrects oneself.

8 On language in its broad sense, see Taylor (1975: 382).

9 Thus Barber argues that we should 'give each citizen some control over what the community will mean by the crucial terms it uses to define all the citizens' selves' (Barber 1984: 193).

10 Cf. Elster (1986). See also Miller (1989: ch. 10) and Miller (1992).

11 In the next chapter I discuss and reject the idea that communities are constituted by hatred of the foreigner.

12 One's notion of one's identity is related to conceptions of time in general. This means that our development from a *tabula rasa* to an adult takes place in connection with time, that we define ourselves in terms of time, and that we understand ourselves in relation to time. There are a few psychological theories that support this claim. Green (1975) writes: 'People who are disoriented in their former relation to time are maladjusted, for they have no past time. Amnesia for time cripples the self, causing it to feel empty and unable to function in the present.' See also Ruddock (1972), Rabin (1975) and Holmes Rolston III (1981).

13 I shall not go into detail and discuss the many metaphysical theories of what personal unity is. To the interested reader I recommend Vesey's book (1974) as a brief summary and analysis. For the question of the unity of the self as it is described here, see especially pp. 7–8.

14 See also Hilgard *et al.* (1971: 414–18).

15 Chekhov A., *Three Sisters* in *Four Plays*, trans. by David Magarshack, N.Y., Hill and Wang, 1969, Act I, p. 126. My attention was drawn to these lines by T. Ball's paper (1985) (whose thesis, albeit very interesting, I totally reject).

16 In 1984 I visited the village of Urgup in Turkey and was present at the annual vintage celebration. Suddenly the mayor stopped the ceremony

and said something to the people standing beside him. Somebody ran into an adjacent house and returned carrying a statue of Mustapha Kemal. 'Now that Ataturk is with us', the mayor announced, 'we can go on with the ceremony.'

17 Plato, *Symposium*, ed. K. Dover, Cambridge: Cambridge University Press, St. 207–8.
18 I am indebted to Gabriel Cohen for his comments.
19 This is especially true for the various elites.
20 Cf. Menuchin and Menuchin (1985). I should mention that this picture is, again, particularly true with respect to the various elites.
21 For instance, Nietzsche (1956).
22 See, for example, Euben (1990), in which classical theory is discussed in the light of contemporary political and moral dilemmas.

2 APPLICATIONS OF THE THEORY

1 Sen (1961). For a variety of attitudes towards discounting the future, see Attfield and Dell (1989), Goodin (1982), Parfit (1984: 480–486), Pearce *et al.* (1989).
2 Taking for granted that a nation is a community – indeed, a trans-generational one (a nation, of course, is not the only form of trans-generational community).
3 Taylor gives the example of public religious practices that have suffered this fate. He thinks of societies such as Spain, which is officially Catholic, while many of its citizens describe themselves as anti-clerical.
4 Cf Ellis (1991) and Schwarzenbach (1991).
5 My distinction between the transgenerational community and the more remote future generations should not be confused with the distinction between the community of one's birth and what has been called the community of humanity, for two reasons. First, the obligations to remote future generations which are based on the demands of humanity are *not* a matter of justice, whereas a community is an institution that entails obligations of justice. Second, the transgenerational community is not necessarily a community into which one was born, nor is it necessarily a nation. It is a community from which one derives one's values and norms, and thus can be an academic community, a party, an international organization, a religion, or an ideological movement as well as a nation. Moreover, one can join it at any stage of one's life: it need not be one's community of birth.

3 THE UTILITARIAN THEORY AND THE NOT-YET-BORN

1 Utilitarian environmentalists may refer to the utilities of non-human animals in this ecosystem as well. See, for instance, the works of Peter Singer.
2 This example was originally suggested by Parfit, and discussed again by Narveson (1976) and Singer (1976a).

3 This is a delicate issue. Following several papers on euthanasia (e.g. 1979) Peter Singer (1992) reported some quite intolerant reactions.

4 I call it a paradox although some would not consider it as one. On this issue see Parfit (1976, 1982, 1983).

5 Jerome K. Jerome, *Three Men in a Boat*, first published in 1889. The quotation is from the edition published by Alan Sutton Publishing, 1983, p. 72.

6 Fifty-five per cent of the members of *De Groenen* party in the Netherlands declared that they would prefer the survival of nature to the survival of man if they had to choose between the two. See Lucardie *et al.* (1993: 54).

7 For similar arguments about the tactics of Green political theory see Goodin (1992).

8 In addition, it has been argued, such a policy fails to distinguish between obligations that have to do with distributional transfers and obligations of compensatory transfers. The latter are thus disregarded. See Spash (1993).

4 CONTRACTARIAN THEORIES OF INTERGENERATIONAL JUSTICE

1 Barry himself discusses Rawls's theory of intergenerational justice in this book (1989: 190–203). For other works by Barry about intergenerational justice and obligations to future generations, see the Bibliography.

2 Rawls (1973: 126; 1958). This is an adaptation of Hume's doctrine.

3 See Gauthier (1977), who says that mutual hostility characterizes political societies. To use Hobbes's words, 'Covenants, without the sword, are but words'. For an interesting discussion of Gauthier and Hobbesian morality, see Hannaford (1988).

4 After Schelling (1978).

5 There is a lot of literature about the strategy of choosing behind the veil of ignorance; however, the maximin strategy suits the intergenerational context very well. Indeed, its attractiveness is in situations marked by certain special features: knowledge of likelihoods is impossible; it is not worthwhile for the person choosing to take a chance for the sake of a further advantage, especially when it may turn out that he loses much that is important to him; and the rejected alternatives have outcomes that one can hardly accept (Rawls 1973: 154). Not only do these features not change, but they are even more obvious in the intergenerational context. So it seems that any rational person with average knowledge about environmental time bombs would choose according to the maximin strategy.

6 Singer B. A. (1988) suggested modifying the original position so that the theory generates an environmental rights ethic. I discuss this attempt elsewhere (de-Shalit 1994).

7 Notice that Rawls refers to later generations of the least advantaged, whereas our intuitions, I believe, are that many obligations, especially those concerning the environment, are to *all* future people.

8 This assumption drew criticism from feminist scholars, e.g. Susan Okin

(1987) and Carol Pateman (1980). Elsewhere Rawls notes that heads of families could also be mothers. See Rawls (1975a: 537).

9 See, for example, Barber (1975), Fisk (1975), MacPherson (1973), Nagel (1975), and Schwartz (1973).

10 For a further discussion of future people's preferences and tastes, and how we are unable to predict them, see Cacharan and Bodde (1983).

11 Rawls (1980, 1982), and recently Rawls (1993: 19, 29–35).

12 Although it has been argued recently that Rawls puts forward an 'enlightened communitarianism'. See Schwarzenbach (1991).

13 See also Rawls's discussion of moral education, sections 70, 71 (1973; 1993: 199–200); compare with Schrag (1976).

14 A slightly different revision of the original position was suggested by Elliot (1985). It was challenged by Attfield (1987: 10–11; 1991: ch. 6).

5 RIGHTS OF FUTURE PEOPLE

1 For a discussion of a rights-based morality in general see Raz (1986: Ch. 8), Dworkin (1977), Mackie (1978), and Freeden (1991).

2 Compare J. S. Mill, (1954, Ch. 1), who did not accept that children had rights, with Feinberg (1980a: 178).

3 I am indebted to Andrew Brennan for suggesting this distinction as a fruitful approach.

4 I discuss the two interpretations elsewhere (1992b).

5 For further reading on neutrality see Goodin and Reeve (1989).

6 I discuss this more profoundly in the next chapter, and elaborate on it in two papers. One asks what kind of Green ideology is liberal (1992d), and the other what kind of liberalism is Green (1993).

7 Goodin (1988: 180) uses a similar argument in relation to the present and the past. David Miller (1989: 308) notes that the level of welfare claims is a function of economic capacity.

8 It is arguable that sometimes human rights may also (although not necessarily) be based on individuals in their social contexts. See Freeden (1990).

6 SUMMARY AND OPEN QUESTIONS

1 On Buddhism and relations with future generations, see Bickham (1981). On environmental ethics and Buddhism see also Rolston III (1989) and *Philosophy East and West*, vol. 37, no. 2 (1987), which is dedicated to the Asian traditions as a conceptual resource for environmental ethics. See also Kealey (1990).

2 The 'forum' model allows us to abandon our previous ideas in the course of a debate. Nevertheless, the difference between this and the market model is that in the former this debate reflects a change in my 'self': I no longer believe that x is right, but rather that y is. And yet the belief in y is now a part of me, of what my 'self' is.

3 See also Mark Sagoff's attempt to reconcile environmentalism and liberalism (1988: 146–70). But see also de-Shalit (1993) where I argue that

the only liberalism which ties in with environmentalism is the non-individualistic version of liberalism.

4 I shall not discuss this point any further. The reader may refer to Rolston (1986: 118–42, 180–205), and Leopold (1949: 188), or, for a different perspective, to Nash (1982: 270).

5 This term is used by Pearce *et al.* (1989).

6 Following the debate between the north and the south in Rio 1992, the Indians issued an alternative programme. See the doctrine of the Centre for Science and Environment, published in *Alternatives*, 17 (1992: 261–79).

7 According to the Greenpeace reports 95 per cent of toxic materials are produced in West Europe, the United States and Japan. In 1989 the Basel Convention on the Control of Transboundary Movements of Hazardous Wastes and their Disposal was signed, but it was not enough to prevent this exportation.

BIBLIOGRAPHY

Ackerman B. (1980) *Social Justice in the Liberal State*, New Haven: Yale University Press.

Anderson F. R. (ed.) (1977), *Environmental Improvement Through Economic Incentives*, Baltimore and London: Johns Hopkins University Press.

Arrow K. J. (1973) 'Rawls's principles of just savings', *Swedish Journal of Economics*, vol. 75: 323–35.

Ashby E. (1980) 'The search for an environmental ethic', *The Tanner Lectures on Human Values*, Salt Lake City, Utah: University of Utah Press.

Attfield R. (1987) *A Theory of Value and Obligation*, London: Croom Helm.

Attfield R. (1991) *The Ethics of Environmental Concern* (2nd edn), Athens, Ga.: University of Georgia Press.

Attfield R. and K. Dell (eds) (1989) *Values, Conflict and the Environment*, Ian Ramsey Centre, Oxford, and the Centre for Applied Ethics, Cardiff.

Avineri S. and A. de-Shalit (1992) *Communitarianism and Individualism*, Oxford: Oxford University Press.

Baier A. (1981) 'The rights of past and future persons' in E. Partridge (ed.) *Responsibilities to Future Generations*, Buffalo: Prometheus Books.

Baier K. (1981) 'When does the right to life begin?' in J. R. Pennock and J. W. Chapman (eds) *Nomos XXIII, Human Rights*, New York: New York University Press.

Ball T. (1985) 'The incoherence of intergenerational justice', *Inquiry*, vol. 28: 321–38.

Barber B. (1975) 'Justifying justice: problems of psychology, politics and measurement in Rawls', *American Political Science Review*, vol. 69: 663–75.

Barber B. (1984) *Strong Democracy: Participatory Politics for a New Age*, Berkeley and Los Angeles: University of California Press.

Barry B. (1973) *The Liberal Theory of Justice*, Oxford: Clarendon Press.

Barry, B. (1977a) 'Justice between generations' in P.M.S. Hacker and J. Raz (eds) *Law, Morality and Society*, Oxford: Clarendon Press.

Barry B. (1977b) 'Rawls on average and total utility: a comment', *Philosophical Studies*, vol. 31: 317–25.

Barry B. (1978) 'Circumstances of justice and future generations' in R. I. Sikora and B. Barry (eds) *Obligations to Future Generations*, Philadelphia, Pa.: Temple University Press.

Barry B. (1979) 'Justice as reciprocity' in E. Kamenka and A. Tay (eds) *Ideas and Ideologies; Justice*, New York: St Martin's Press, pp. 50–78.

Barry B. (1982) 'Humanity and justice in global perspective' in J. R. Pennock and J. W. Chapman (eds) *Nomos XXIV, Ethics Economics and the Law*, New Haven: Yale University Press, pp. 219–52; reprinted as 'Humanity and justice' in his (1989) *Democracy, Power and Justice*, Oxford: Clarendon Press.

Barry B. (1983a) 'Self government revisited' in D. Miller and L. Siedentrop (eds) *The Nature of Political Theory*, Oxford: Clarendon Press.

Barry B. (1983b) 'Intergenerational justice in energy policy' in D. MacLean (ed.) *Energy and the Future*, Totowa, NJ: Rowman and Littlefield.

Barry B. (1989) *Theories of Justice*, London: Harvester Wheatsheaf.

Bates S. (1974) 'The motivation to be just', *Ethics*, vol. 85: 1–17.

Bayles M. (ed.) (1976) *Ethics and Population*, Cambridge, Mass.: Schenkman

Becker L. C. (1986) *Reciprocity*, London and New York: Routledge and Kegan Paul.

Benhabib S. (1981) 'Liberal dialogue versus a critical theory of discursive' in N. Rosenblaum (ed.) *Liberalism and the Moral Life*, Cambridge, Mass.: Harvard University Press, pp. 143–56.

Bennet J. (1978) 'On maximizing happiness' in R. Sikora and B. Barry (eds) *Obligations to Future Generations*, Philadelphia, Pa.: Temple University Press.

Bentham J. (1948 (1780)) *The Principles of Moral and Legal Legislation*, New York: Hafner Books.

Bickham S. (1981) 'Future generations and contemporary ethical theory', *Journal of Value Inquiry*, vol. 15 (2): 169–77.

Blackstone T. (ed.) (1974) *Philosophy and Environmental Crisis*, Athens, Ga.: University of Georgia Press.

Bloom A. (1975) 'Justice: John Rawls vs political philosophy', *American Political Science Review*, vol. 69: 648–63.

Brennan A. (1984) 'The moral standing of natural objects', *Environmental Ethics*, vol. 6: 35–6.

Brennan A. (1988) *Thinking About Nature*, Athens, Ga.: University of Georgia Press.

Brennan A. (1992) 'Moral pluralism and the environment', *Environmental Values*, vol. 1: 15–33.

Cacharan T. B. and D. L. Bodde (1983) 'Conflicting views on a neutrality criterion for radioactive waste management' in D. MacLean (ed.) *Energy and the Future*, Totowa, NJ: Rowman and Littlefield.

Callahan D. (1981) 'What obligations do we have to future generations?' in E. Partridge (ed.) *Responsibilities to Future Generations*, New York: Prometheus Books.

Cameron J.R. (1989) 'Do future generations matter?' in N. Dower (ed.) *Ethics and Environmental Responsibility*, Aldershot: Averbury.

Care N. S. (1982) 'Future generations, public policy and the motivation problem', *Environmental Ethics*, vol. 4: 195–213.

Carrithers S. and S. Lukes (eds) (1985) *The Category of the Person*, Cambridge: Cambridge University Press.

Clark S. R. L. (1977) *The Moral Status of Animals*, Oxford: Oxford University Press.

Clark S. R. L. (1986) 'Icons, sacred relics, obsolescent plant', *Journal of Applied Philosophy*, vol. 3: 201–10

Coleman J. L. (1985) 'Market contractarianism and the unanimity rule' in E. F. Paul, J. Paul and F. D. Miller (eds) *Ethics and Economics*, Oxford: Basil Blackwell.

Craig L. H. (1975) 'Contra contact: a brief against John Rawls's theory of justice', *Canadian Journal of Political Science*, vol. 8: 63–82.

Dahrendorf R. (1969) *Society and Democracy in Germany*, New York: Anchor Books.

Daniels N. (ed.) (1975) *Reading Rawls*, Oxford: Blackwell.

De George, R. (1979) 'The environment, rights and future generations' in K. E. Goodpaster and K. M. Sayre (eds) *Ethics and Problems of the 21st Century*, Notre Dame: University of Notre Dame Press.

DeLattre E. (1972) 'Rights, responsibilities and future generations', *Ethics*, vol. 82: 254–8.

DeLone R. H. (1977) *Small Future: Children, Inequality and Limits of Liberal Reform*, New York: Harcourt Brace Jovanovich.

Derr T. S. (1981) 'The obligations to the future' in E. Partridge (ed.) *Responsibilities to Future Generations*, Buffalo: Prometheus Books.

Devos A., N. Pearson, P. Silveston and W. R. Drynan (eds) (1986) *The Pollution Reader*, Montreal: Harvest House.

Dobson A. (1990) *Green Political Thought*, London: Harper and Collins.

Dworkin R. (1977) *Taking Rights Seriously*, London: Duckworth.

Dworkin R. (1985) *A Matter of Principle*, Oxford: Oxford University Press.

Dworkin R. (1986) *Law's Empire*, London: Fontana Press.

Eckersley R. (1992) 'Green versus ecosocialist economic programmes', *Political Studies*, vol. 40: 315–33.

Ehrenfeld D. (1978) *The Arrogance of Humanism*, New York: Oxford University Press.

Elliot R. (1985) 'Critical notice of the ethics of environmental concern', *Australian Journal of Philosophy*, vol. 63: 499–509.

Elliot R. (1989) 'The rights of future people', *Journal of Applied Philosophy*, vol. 6: 159–71.

Ellis R. D. (1991) 'Towards a reconciliation of liberalism and communitarianism', *Journal of Value Inquiry*, vol. 25: 55–64.

Elster J. (1979) 'Risk, uncertainty and nuclear power' in *Social Sciences Information*, vol. 18; reprinted in J. Elster (1983) *Explaining Technical Change*, Cambridge: Cambridge University Press.

Elster J. (1984) *Ulysses and the Sirens*, Cambridge: Cambridge University Press.

Elster J. (1986) 'The market and the forum: three varieties of political theory' in J. Elster and A. Hylland (eds) *The Foundations of Social Choice Theory*, Cambridge: Cambridge University Press.

English J. (1977) 'Justice between generations', *Philosophical Studies*, vol. 31: 91–104.

Euben J. P. (1990) *The Tragedy of Political Theory: The Road Not Taken*, Princeton, N.J.: Princeton University Press.

Feinberg J. (1980a) 'The rights of animals and future generations', in his *Rights, Justice and the Bounds of Liberty*, Princeton, N.J.: Princeton University Press, pp. 159–85.

Feinberg J. (1980b) 'The nature and value of rights' in *Rights, Justice and the Bounds of Liberty*, Princeton, N.J. Princeton University Press, pp.143–58.

Feinberg J. (1980c) 'Is there a right to be born?' in *Rights, Justice and the Bounds of Liberty*, Princeton, N.J. Princeton University Press, pp. 207–20.

Fisk M. (1975) 'History and reason in Rawls' moral theory' in N. Daniels (ed.) *Reading Rawls*, Oxford: Blackwell.

Frankena K.W. (1974) 'Ethics and the environment' in K. E. Goodpaster and K. M. Sayre (eds) *Ethics and Problems of the 21st Century*, Notre Dame: University of Notre Dame Press.

Freeden M. (1990) 'Human rights and welfare', *Ethics*, vol. 100: 489–503.

Freeden M. (1991) *Rights*, Milton Keynes: Open University Press.

Galston W. A. (1989) 'Pluralism and social unity', *Ethics*, vol. 99: 711–26.

Gauthier D. (1977) 'The social contract as ideology', *Philosophy and Public Affairs*, vol. 6: 130–64.

Gauthier D. (1978a) 'Social choice and distributive justice', *Philosophia*, vol. 7: 239–53.

Gauthier D. (1978b) 'Morality and advantage' in J. Raz (ed.) *Practical Morality*, Oxford: Oxford University Press.

Gauthier D. (1985) 'Bargaining and justice' in E. F. Paul, J. Paul and F. D. Miller (eds), *Ethics and Economics*, Oxford: Blackwell.

Gauthier D. (1986) *Morals By Agreement*, Oxford: Clarendon Press.

Gibbard A. (1989) 'Communities and judgement', *Social Philosophy and Policy*, vol. 7: 175–89.

Glover J. (1979) 'How should we decide what sort of world is best?' in K. E. Goodpaster and K. M. Sayre (eds) *Ethics and Problems of the 21st Century*, Notre Dame: University of Notre Dame Press, pp. 79–92.

Golding M. P. (1968) 'Towards a theory of human rights', *Monist*, vol. 52.

Golding M. P. (1972) 'Obligations to future generations', *Monist*, vol. 56: 85–99; reprinted in E. Partridge (ed.) (1981) *Responsibilities to Future Generations*, Buffalo: Prometheus Books.

Golding M. P. (1978) 'Future generations – obligations to', *Encyclopedia of Bioethics*, vol. 2, New York: Macmillan.

Golding M. P. and N. H. Golding (1979) 'Why preserve landmarks? a preliminary inquiry', in K. E. Goodpaster (ed.) *Ethics and Problems of the 21st Century*, Notre Dame: University of Notre Dame Press.

Goodin R. (1978) 'Uncertainty as an excuse for cheating our children: the case of nuclear wastes', *Policy Sciences*, vol. 10: 25–45.

Goodin R. (1982) 'Discounting discounting', *Journal of Public Policy*, vol. 2: 53–72.

Goodin R. (1985) *Protecting the Vulnerable*, Chicago, Ill.: University of Chicago Press.

Goodin R. (1988) *Reasons for Welfare*, Princeton, N.J.: Princeton University Press.

Goodin R. (1992a) *Green Political Theory*, Oxford: Polity.

147

Goodin R. (1992b) *Motivating Political Morality*, Oxford: Blackwell.

Goodin R. and A. Reeve (eds) (1989) *Liberal Neutrality*, London: Routledge.

Goodpaster K. E. (1978) 'On being morally considerable', *Journal of Philosophy*, vol. 75: 308–25.

Goodpaster K. E. and K. M. Sayre (eds) (1979) *Ethics and Problems of the 21st Century*, Notre Dame: University of Notre Dame Press.

Govier T. (1979) 'What should we do about future people?', *American Philosophical Quarterly*, vol. 16: 105–13.

Green H. B. (1975) 'Aging: temporal stages in the development of the self' in J. T. Fraser and N. Lawrence (eds) *The Study of Time*, vol. II, Berlin, Heidelberg, New York: Springer-Verlag.

Green R. M. (1977) 'Intergenerational distributive justice and environmental responsibility', *Bioscience*; reprinted in E. Partridge (ed.) (1981) *Responsibilities to Future Generations*, Buffalo: Prometheus Books.

Gutmann A. (1985) 'Communitarian critics of liberalism', *Philosophy and Public Affairs*, vol. 14: 308–22.

Hannaford R.V. (1988) 'Gauthier, Hobbes and Hobbesians', *International Journal of Moral and Social Studies*, vol. 3: 239–55.

Hanser M. (1990) 'Harming future people', *Philosophy and Public Affairs*, vol. 19: 47–90.

Hardin G. (1968) 'The tragedy of the commons', *Science*, vol. 162: 1243–8.

Hardin G. (1977) 'Living on a lifeboat' in G. Hardin and J. Baden (eds) *Managing the Commons*, San Francisco, Calif: W.H.Freeman, pp. 261–79.

Hardin G. (1981) 'Who cares for posterity?' in E. Partridge (ed.) *Responsibilities to Future Generations*, Buffalo: Prometheus Books.

Hare R. M. (1973) 'Rawls's theory of justice', *Philosophical Quarterly*, vol. 23: 241–52.

Hare R. M. (1981) *Moral Thinking*, Oxford: Clarendon Press.

Hargrove E. (1988) *Foundations of Environmental Ethics*, Englewood Cliffs, N.J.: Prentice-Hall.

Hart H. L. A. (1982) *Essays on Bentham; Jurisprudence and Political Theory*, Oxford: Clarendon Press.

Hartmann N. (1932) *Ethics, II (Moral Values)*, New York: Macmillan.

Herman B. (1992) 'Pluralism and the community of moral judgment', unpublished paper delivered at the Jerusalem Philosophical Encounter, December.

Heyd D. (1988) 'Procreation and value: can ethics deal with futurity problems', *Philosophia*, vol. 18: 151–70.

Heyd D. (1992) *Genethics*, Berkeley, Calif.: University of California Press.

Hilgard E., Ric. Atkinson Rit. Atkinson (eds) (1971) *Introduction to Psychology*, 5th edn, New York: Harcourt Brace Jovanovich.

Hospers J. (1972) *Human Conduct*, New York: Harcourt Brace Jovanovich.

Hubin D. C. (1975) 'The scope of justice', *Philosophy and Public Affairs*, vol. 5: 274–93.

Hubin D. C. (1976) 'Justice and future generations', *Philosophy and Public Affairs*, vol. 6. 70–83.

Hugh H. M. (1973) 'Our concern with others' in A. Montefiore (ed.) *Philosophy and Personal Relations*, London: Routledge and Kegan Paul.

Huxley J. (1956) 'World population', *Scientific American*, March.

Johnson L. E. (1991) *A Morally Deep World*, Cambridge: Cambridge University Press.

Jonas H. (1984) *The Imperative of Responsibility*, Chicago, Ill.: Chicago University Press.

Kahn H. (1977) *The Next 200 Years*, London: Associated Business Programmes.

Kavka G. (1978) 'The futurity problem' in R. I. Sikora and B. Barry (eds) *Obligations to Future Generations*, Philadelphia, Pa.: Temple University Press.

Kavka G. (1982) 'The paradox of future individuals', *Philosophy and Public Affairs*, vol. 11: 93–112.

Kavka G. (1986) *Hobbesian Moral and Political Theory*, Princeton, N.J.: Princeton University Press.

Kealey D. A. (1990) *Revisioning Environmental Ethics*, Albany, N.Y.: SUNY Press.

Keat R. and D. Miller (1974) 'Understanding justice', *Political Theory*, vol. 2: 3–37.

Ketab G. (1989) 'Democratic individuality and the meaning of rights' in N. Rosenblaum (ed.) *Liberalism and the Moral Life*, Cambridge, Mass.: Harvard University Press, pp. 183–206.

Laslett P. (1979) 'The conversation between generations' in P. Laslett and J. Fishkin (eds) *Philosophy, Politics and Society*, 5th series, Oxford: Blackwell.

Leopold A. (1949) *A Sand County Almanac*, New York: Oxford Unversity Press.

Lessnoff M. (1971) 'John Rawls's theory of justice', *Political Studies*, vol. 19: 63–81.

Lucardie P., G. Voerman and W. van Schuur (1993) 'Different shades of green: a comparison between members of *Groen Links* and *De Groenen*', *Environmental Politics*, vol. 2: 40–62.

Lukes S. (1989) 'Making sense of moral conflict' in N. Rosenblaum (ed.) *Liberalism and the Moral Life*, Cambridge, Mass.: Harvard University Press.

MacIntyre A. (1981) *After Virtue*, London: Duckworth.

MacKenzie M. (1985) 'A note on motivation and future generations', *Environmental Ethics*, vol. 7: 63–70.

Mackie J. L. (1978) 'Can there be a right based moral theory?' in *Midwest Studies in Philosophy*, vol. 3, Minneapolis, Minn.: University of Minnesota Press.

Macklin R. (1981) 'Can future generations correctly be said to have rights?' in E. Partridge (ed.) *Responsibilities to Future Generations*, Buffalo: Prometheus Books.

Maclean D. (1983) 'A moral requirement for energy policies' in D. MacLean and P. Brown (eds) *Energy and the Future*, Totowa, N.J.: Rowman and Littlefield.

MacLean D. and P. Brown (eds) (1983) *Energy and the Future*, Totowa, N.J.: Rowman and Littlefield.

MacMahan J. (1981) 'Problems of population policy', *Ethics*, vol. 92: 96–128.

MacPherson C. B. (1973) 'Rawls' model of man and society', *Philosophy and Social Sciences*, vol. 3: 341–7.

Manning R. (1981) 'Environmental ethics and Rawls's theory of justice', *Environmental Ethics*, vol. 3: 155–65.

May J. (1989) *Nuclear Age*, London: Victor Gollancz.

Menuchin D. and I. Menuchin (eds) (1985) *The Limits of Obedience* (in Hebrew), Tel-Aviv: Siman Kria and Yesh Gvul ("There is a Border") movement.

Mill J. S. (1900) *Principles of Political Economy*, New York: Coloural Press.

Mill, J.S. (1954 [1910]) *On Liberty*, London: J.M. Dent.

Miller D. (1976) *Social Justice*, Oxford: Clarendon Press.

Miller D. (1984) *Anarchism*, London and Melbourne: J. M. Dent.

Miller D. (1988) 'The ethical significance of nationality', *Ethics*, vol. 98: 647–63.

Miller D. (1989) *Market, State and Community*, Oxford: Clarendon Press.

Miller D. (1992) 'Deliberative democracy and social choice', *Political Studies*, vol. 40, Special Issue: 54–67.

Miller H. B. and W. H. Williams (eds) (1982) *The Limits of Utilitarianism*, Minneapolis, Minn.: University of Minnesota Press.

Moberg D. (1991) 'The environment and the market', *Dissent,*: 511–19.

Morris C. W. (1988) 'The relation between self-interest and justice in contractarian ethics', in *Social Philosophy and Policy*; 'Gauthier's New Social Contract', vol. 5: 119–53.

Murphy P. (1992) 'Rethinking the relation of nature, culture and agency', *Environmental Values*, vol. 1: 311–20.

Nagel T. (1975) 'Rawls on justice' in N. Daniels, *Reading Rawls*, Oxford: Blackwell.

Nagel T. (1981) 'Death' in *Mortal Questions*, Cambridge: Cambridge University Press.

Narveson J. (1967) 'Utilitarianism and new generations', *Mind*, vol. 76: 62–72.

Narveson J. (1976) 'Moral problems of population' in M. D. Bayles (ed.) *Ethics and Population*, Cambridge, Mass.: Schenkman.

Narveson J. (1977) 'Animal rights', *Canadian Journal of Philosophy*, vol. 7: 161–78.

Narveson J. (1978) 'Future people and us', in R. I. Sikora and B. Barry (eds) *Obligations to Future Generations*, Philadelphia, Pa.: Temple University Press.

Nash J. F. (1950) 'The bargaining problem', *Econometrica*, vol. 18: 155–62.

Nash R. (1982) *Wilderness in the American Mind*, New Haven, Conn.: Yale University Press.

Nash R. (1989) *The Rights of Nature*, Madison, Wis.: University of Wisconsin Press.

Nietzsche F. (1956) *The Birth of Tragedy*, Garden City, N.Y.: Doubleday.

Norman R. (1983) *The Moral Philosophers*, Oxford: Clarendon Press.

Norton B. G. (1982) 'Environment, ethics and the rights of future generations', *Environmetnal Ethics*, vol. 4: 319–38.

Nozick R. (1974) *Anarchy, State and Utopia*, Oxford: Basil Blackwell.

Okin S. (1987) 'Justice and gender', *Philosophy and Public Affairs*, vol. 16: 42–72.

Ophulos W. (1977) *Ecology and the Politics of Scarcity*, San Francisco, Calif.: Freeman.

O'riordan T. (1991) 'Stability and transformation in environmental government', *The Political Quarterly*, vol. 62: 167–84.

Paehlke R. (1989) *Environmentalism and the Future of Progressive Politics*, New Haven, Conn.: Yale University Press.

Paehlke R. (1990) 'Environmental values and democracy' in N. Vig and M. Kraft (eds), *Environmental Policies in the 1990s*, Washington, D.C.: CO Press.

Page T. (1983) 'Intergenerational justice as opportunity' in D. MacLean and P. Brown (eds) *Energy and the Future*, Totowa, N.J.: Rowman and Littlefield.

Parfit D. (1971) 'On the importance of self identity', *Journal of Philosophy*, vol. 68: 683–90.

Parfit D. (1973) 'Later selves and moral principles' in A. Montefiore (ed.) *Philosophy and Personal Relations*, London: Routledge and Kegan Paul, pp. 137–70.

Parfit D. (1976) 'On doing the best for our children' in M. Bayles (ed.) *Ethics and Population*, Cambridge, Mass.: Schenkman, pp. 100–18.

Parfit D. (1982) 'Future generations: further problems', *Philosophy and Public Affaits*, vol. 11: 113–73.

Parfit D. (1983) 'Energy policy and further future: the social discount rate' in D. MacLean and P. Brown (eds) *Energy and the Future*, Totowa, N.J.: Rowman and Littlefield; reprinted in Parfit D. (1984), *Reasons and Persons*: 480–6.

Parfit D. (1984) *Reasons and Persons*, Oxford: Clarendon Press.

Partridge E. (ed.) (1981a) *Responsibilities to future Generations*, Buffalo: Prometheus Books.

Partridge E. (1981b) 'Why care about the future' in E. Partridge (ed.) *Responsibilities to Future Generations*, Buffalo: Prometheus Books.

Partridge E. (1981c) 'Posthumous interests and posthumous respect', *Ethics*, vol. 91: 243–64.

Passmore J. (1974) *Man's Responsibility for Nature*, London: Duckworth.

Pateman C. (1980) 'The disorder of women: women, love and the sense of justice', *Ethics*, vol. 91: 20–34; reprinted in C. Pateman (1989) *The Disorder of Women*, Oxford: Polity Press.

Pearce D., A. Markandya and E. Barbier (1989) *Blueprint for a Green Economy*, London: Earthscan.

Pendiville B. (1992) 'The French greens inside out', *Environmental Politics*, vol. 1: 282–7.

Plant R. (1978) 'Community: concept, conception and ideology', *Politics and Society*, vol. 8: 79–107.

Pletcher G. K. (1980) 'The rights of future generations' in E. Partridge (ed.) *Responsibilities to Future Generations*, Buffalo: Prometheus Books.

Pollock P.H. and S.A. Lillie (1992) 'Who says it's risky business?', *Polity*, vol. 24: 449–513.

Porritt J. (1984) *Seeing Green*, Oxford: Basil Blackwell.

Porter G. and J. Brown (1991) *Global Environmental Politics*, Boulder, Colo.: Westview Press.

Rabin A. I. (1975) 'Future time perspective and ego strength' in J. Fraser and N. Lawrence (eds) *The Study of Time*, vol. II, Berlin, Heidelberg, New York: Springer-Verlag.

Rachels J. (1991) *Created From Animals*, Oxford: Oxford University Press.

Rapoport E. (1977) 'Classical liberalism and Rawls revisionism', *Canadian Journal of Philosophy*; supplementary, vol III: 95–120.

Rawls J. (1958) 'Justice as fairness', *Philosophical Review*, vol. 62.

Rawls J. (1967) 'Distributive justice' in P. Laslett and W.G. Runchiman (eds) *Philosophy, Politics and Society*, 3rd series, Oxford: Basil Blackwell.

Rawls J. (1973) *Theory of Justice*, Oxford: Oxford University Press.

Rawls J. (1975a) 'Fairness to goodness', *Philosophical Review*, vol. 84: 536–54.

Rawls J. (1975b) 'A Kantian conception of equity', *The Cambridge Review*, vol. 96: 94–9.

Rawls J. (1980) 'Kantian constructivism in moral theory: the Dewey lectures 1980', *Journal of Philosophy*, vol. 77: 515–72.

Rawls J. (1982) 'Social unity and primary goods' in A. Sen and B. Williams (eds) *Utilitarianism and Beyond*, Cambridge: Cambridge University Press.

Rawls J. (1985) 'Justice as fairness: political not metaphysical', *Philosophy and Public Affairs*, vol. 14: 223–51.

Rawls J. (1993) *Political Liberalism*, New York: Columbia University Press.

Raz J. (1986) *The Morality of Freedom*, Oxford: Clarendon Press.

Regan T. (1982) *All that Dwell Therein: Animal Rights and Environmental Ethics*, Berkeley, Calif: University of California Press.

Regan T. (1983) *The Case for Animal Rights*, Berkeley, Calif: University of California Press.

Renner M.G. (1991) 'Forgoing enviromental alliances', *World Watch*, November-December: 8–15.

Richards D. A. J. (1971) *Theory of Reason of Action*, Oxford: Clarendon Press.

Richards D. A. J. (1980) 'Human rights and moral ideas: an essay on the moral theory of liberalism' in *Social Theory and Practice*, vol. 5 (3–4): 461–88.

Richards D. A. J. (1983) 'Contractarian theory, intergenerational justice and energy policy' in D. MacLean and P. Brown (eds) *Energy and the Future*, Totowa, N.J.: Rowman and Littlefield.

Rollin B.E. (1981) *Animal Rights and Human Morlaity*, Buffalo: Prometheus Books.

Rolston III H. (1981) 'The river of life: past, present, future' in E. Partridge (ed.) *Responsibilities to Future Generations*, Buffalo: Prometheus Books.

Rolston III H. (1986) *Philosophy Gone Wild*, Buffalo: Prometheus Books.

Rolston III H. (1988) *Environmental Ethics*, Philadelphia, Pa.: Temple University Press.

Rolston III H. (1989) 'Zen Buddhism today', Annual report of the Kyoto Zen Symposium, September.

Rorty R. (1988) 'The priority of democracy to philosophy' in M. Petterson and R. vaughan (eds), *The Virgina State of Religious Feelings*, Madison, Wis.: University of Wisconsin Press.

Roth A. E. (1981) 'Sociological versus strategic factors in bargaining', *Journal of Economic Behaviour and Organization*, vol. 2: 174–7.

Rothenberg D. (1992) 'Individual or community? two approaches to ecophilosophy in practice', *Environmental Values*, vol. 1: 123–32.

Routley V. and R. Routley (1978) 'Nuclear energy and obligations to future generations', *Inquiry*, vol. 21: 133–79.

Ruddock R. (1972) *Six Approaches to the Person*, London: Routledge and Kegan Paul.

Sagoff M. (1988) *The Economy of the Earth*, Cambridge: Cambridge University Press.

Sandel M. (1982) *Liberalism and the Limits of Justice*, Cambridge: Cambridge University Press.

Sandel M. (ed.) (1984a) *Liberalism and Its Critics*, Oxford: Blackwell.

Sandel M. (1984b) 'The procedural republic and the unencumbered self', *Political Theory*, vol. 12: 81–96.

Santayana G. (1955) *The Sense of Beauty*, New York: Random House.

Scanlon T. M. (1982) 'Contractualism and utilitarianism' in A. Sen and B. Williams (eds) *Utilitarianism and Beyond*, Cambridge: Cambridge University Press.

Scheffler S. (ed.) (1988) *Consequentialism and Its Critics*, Oxford: Oxford University Press.

Schelling T. (1978) *Micromotives and Macrobehaviour*, New York: W.W. Norton.

Schrag F. (1976) 'Justice and the family', *Inquiry*, vol. 19.

Schwartz A. (1973) 'Moral neutrality and primary goods', *Ethics*, vol. 83: 294–307.

Schwartz T. (1978) 'Obligations to posterity' in R.I. Sikora and B. Barry (eds) *Obligations to Future Generations*, Philadelphia, Pa.: Temple University Press.

Schwarzenbach S.R. (1991) 'Rawls, Hegel and communitarianism', *Political Theory*, vol. 19: 539–71.

Scott R. Jr (1978) 'Environmental ethics and obligations to future generations' in R.I. Sikora and B. Barry (eds) *Obligations to Future Generations*, Philadelphia, Pa.: Temple University Press.

Seabrook J. (1990) *The Myth of the Market*, London: Green Books.

Sen A. (1961) 'On optimising the saving rate', *Economic Journal*, vol. 71: 479–97.

Sen A. and B. Williams (eds) (1982) *Utilitarianism and Beyond*, Cambridge: Cambridge University Press.

de-Shalit A. (1990) 'Bargaining with the not-yet-born?', *International Journal of Moral and Social Studies*, vol. 5: 221–35.

de-Shalit A. (1992a) 'David Miller's model of market socialism and the recent refoms in the kibbutzim', *Political Studies*, vol. 40: 116–23.

de-Shalit A. (1992b) 'Community and the rights of future generations', *Journal of Applied Philosophy*, vol. 9: 105–17.

de-Shalit A. (1992c) 'Environmental policies and justice between generations', *European Journal of Political Research*, vol. 21: 307–16.

de-Shalit A (1992d) 'Is environmentalism liberal? Two models of two movements', paper delivered at the Israeli Political Science Association annual meeting.

de-Shalit A. (1993) 'European Liberalism and the environment' in B. Brecher and O. Fleischmann (eds.) *Liberalism and the New Europe*, Aldershot: Avebury Press.

de-Shalit A. (1994) 'Urban preservation and the judgement of king Solomon', *Journal of Applied Philosophy*.

Shue H. (1980) *Basic Rights*, Princeton, N.J.: Princeton University Press.

Sidgwick H. (1981) *Methods of Ethics*, Indianapolis, Ind.: Hacket (originally published in 1874).

Sikora R. I. (1979) 'Utilitarianism, supererogation and future generations', *Canadian Journal of Philosophy*, vol. 9: 461–6.

Sikora R. I. and B. Barry (eds) (1978) *Obligations to Future Generations*, Philadelphia, Pa.: Temple University Press.

Singer B.A. (1988) 'An extension of Rawls's theory to environmental ethics', *Environmental Ethics*, vol. 10: 217–31.

Singer P. (1972) 'Famine, affluence and morality', *Philosophy and Public Affairs*, Vol. 1: 229–43. Reprinted in P. Laslett and J. Fishkin (eds) *Philosophy, Politics and Society*, 5th series, Oxford: Blackwell.

Singer P. (1976a) 'A utilitarian population principle' in Bayles M. D. (ed.) *Ethics and Population*, Cambridge, Mass.: Schenkman.

Singer P. (1976b) *Animal Liberation*, London: Jonathan Cape.

Singer P. (1979) *Practical Ethics*, Cambridge: Cambridge University Press.

Singer P. (1992) 'A German attack in applied ethics', *Journal of Applied Philosophy*, vol. 9: 85–92.

Smart J.C.C and B. Williams (1973) *Utilitarianism – For and Against*, Cambridge: Cambridge University Press.

Spash C.L. (1993) 'Economics, ethics, and long-term environmental damages', *Environmental Ethics*, vol. 15: 117–33.

Sprigge T.L.S. (1984) 'Non-human rights: an idealist perspective', *Inquiry*, vol. 27: 439–61.

Stearns J. B. (1972) 'Ecology and the indefinite unborn', *Monist*, vol. 56: 612–25.

Steiner H. (1983) 'The rights of future generations' in D. MacLean (ed.) *Energy and the Future*, Totowa, N.J.: Rowman and Littelefield.

Sterba J. P. (1980) 'Abortion, distant people and future generations', *Journal of Philosophy*, vol. 77: 424–40.

Sterba J. P. (1981) 'The welfare rights of distant people and future generations: moral side-constraints on social policy', *Social Theory and Practice*, vol. 7: 99–120.

Stigler G.J. and G.S. Becker (1977) '*De Gustibus Non Est Disputandum*', *American Economic Review*, vol. 68: 76–90.

Stone C.D. (1972), 'Should trees have standing', *Southern California Law Review*, vol. 45: 450–501.

Sumner L. W. (1978) 'Classical utilitarianism and the problems of population policy' in R.I. Sikora and B. Barry (eds) *Obligations to Future Generations*, Philadelphia, Pa.: Temple University Press.

Surber J. P. (1977) 'Obligations to future generations; explorations and problemata', *Journal of Value Inquiry*, vol. 11: 104–16.

Taylor C. (1975) *Hegel*, Cambridge: Cambridge University Press.

Taylor C. (1985a) *Philosophy and Human Sciences*, Cambridge: Cambridge University Press.

Taylor C. (1985b) 'The person' in S. Carrithers and S. Lukes (eds) *The Category of the Person*, Cambridge: Cambridge University Press.

Taylor P.W. (1986) *Respect for Nature*, Princeton, N.J.: Princeton University Press.

Thompson J. (1990) 'A refuatation of environmental ethics', *Environmental Ethics*, vol. 12: 147–60.

Thomson J. (1992) 'Things in which a thing can be good', *Social Philosophy and Policy*, vol. 9: 96–112.

Vesey G. (1974) *Personal Relations*, Ithaca, N.Y.: Cornell University Press.

Vetter H. (1969), 'The production of children and problems of utilitarian ethics', *Inquiry*, vol. 12: 445–7.

Vetter H. (1971) 'Utilitarianism and new generations', *Mind*, vol. 80: 301–2.

Walzer M. (1970a) 'The obligation to disobey' in *Obligations*, Cambridge, Mass.: Harvard University Press.

Walzer M. (1970b) 'A day in the life of a socialist citizen', *Obligations*, Cambridge, Mass.: Harvard University Press.

Walzer M. (1985) *Spheres of Justice*, Oxford: Blackwell.

Warren M. A. (1977) 'Do potential persons have rights?' *Canadian Journal of Philosophy*; reprinted in R. I. Sikora and B. Barry (eds) (1978) *Obligations to Future Generations*, Philadelphia, Pa.: Temple University Press.

Weiss E. (1986) 'Conservation and equity between generations', a paper delivered in Oxford.

Wenz P. S. (1983) 'Ethics, energy policy and future generations', *Environmental Ethics*, vol. 5: 195–210.

Wenz P.S (1988) *Environmental Justice*, Albany, N.Y.: State of New York University Press.

Whiting J. (1986) 'Friends and future selves', *Philosophical Review*, vol. 95: 547–81.

Williams B. (1991) 'Must concern for the environment be centred on human beings?', a paper delivered at a conference on 'Ethics and the Environment', Corpus Christi College, Oxford, September 1991.

Williams M. B. (1978) 'Discounting versus maximum sustainable yield' in R.I. Sikora and B. Barry (eds) *Obligations to Future Generations*, Philadelphia, Pa.: Temple University Press.

Wolfram S. (1978) 'Morals by agreement', *Philosophical Books*, vol. 28: 129–34.

World Commission on the Environment and Development (1987) *Our Common Future*, Oxford: Oxford University Press.

Young K. (1990) 'Living under threat', in R. Jowell (ed.) *British Social Attitudes*, London: Gower.

INDEX